CAREERS FOR

TRAVEL BUFFS

& Other Restless Types

VGM Careers for You Series

CAREERS FOR

TRAVEL BUFFS

& Other Restless Types

PAUL PLAWIN

SECOND EDITION

VGM Career Books

Chicago   New York   San Francisco   Lisbon   London   Madrid   Mexico City
Milan   New Delhi   San Juan   Seoul   Singapore   Sydney   Toronto

Library of Congress Cataloging-in-Publication Data

Plawin, Paul, 1938–
    Careers for travel buffs & other restless types / Paul Plawin.— 2nd ed.
      p. cm. — (Careers for you series)
    ISBN 0-07-140904-1
      1. Vocational guidance.   2. Travel.   I. Title: Careers for travel buffs and
other restless types.   II. Title: Travel buffs.   III. VGM careers for you series.

    HF5381.P655   2003
    331.7′02—dc21   2002192427

2 3 4 5 6 7 8 9 0   LBM/LBM   2 1 0 9 8 7 6 5 4

ISBN 0-07-140904-1

McGraw-Hill books are available at special quantity discounts to use as premiums
and sales promotions, or for use in corporate training programs. For more
information, please write to the Director of Special Sales, Professional Publishing,
McGraw-Hill, Two Penn Plaza, New York, NY 10121-2298. Or contact your local
bookstore.

This book is printed on acid-free paper.

Contents

Foreword

Since antiquity, people have traveled for exploration, commerce, learning, and pleasure. Tourism liberates the mind and gives us new impressions, new ideas. In the modern world, a global economy has lifted billions of people out of subsistence living and fostered the growth of a worldwide middle class with the discretionary income and desire to visit cultures beyond their own borders.

The travel and tourism industry in the United States employed eighteen million people in 2001. With 95 percent of all travel and tourism businesses qualifying as small businesses, the opportunities are great for new entrepreneurs looking to prove their skills by starting their own companies.

In 2001, the terrorism of September 11 brought great challenges to travelers and the tourism industry. But Americans cling tightly to their precious freedom to travel, and there is every indication that they will continue to do so in the future. History suggests there will be no decrease in our mobility as a nation. Travel has always rebounded quickly after wars and economic recession.

As you explore career possibilities, you will find that in almost every field of work there are jobs in which you can fulfill your quest for traveling. Much of it can be a pleasure. It will surely broaden your horizons.

William S. Norman, President and CEO
Travel Industry Association of America
www.SeeAmerica.org

Acknowledgments

The work of writing books isn't limited to interviews and library research. It relies as well on experiences and information acquired over years through many people. For their savvy ideas, valuable criticism, and pats on the back, I am grateful to my wife, Joan, and children, Jenny and Paul, and colleagues Joyce Lain Kennedy, John and Judy Schulte, Bill Sellers, Hal Gieseking, Carolyn Bennett Patterson, and the late Ralph Danford.

Introduction

I like to travel—always have. I loved Boy Scout camping trips when I was a kid. For someone who grew up where there were sidewalks and apartment buildings, these excursions into the wilderness (now probably suburban residential developments) were exhilarating. Those junky-looking country stores we explored on our overnight hikes were exotic bazaars where we dug into our pockets for change to buy Bazooka bubble gum, cinnamon hot hardball candies, and wine-soaked crook cigars that we smoked surreptitiously when the scoutmasters were out of sight.

Every summer my family visited the relatives 350 miles distant. I always looked forward to these trips—despite memories of getting carsick when we drove too far in the '38 Chevy. During our vacations, we'd manage a side-trip or two. Because my dad and his brother, my Uncle Richard, were interested in Civil War history, we roamed the old battlefields at Petersburg and Antietam and Gettysburg. My memories of these rumpled fields and redoubts are still vivid.

My first trip to New York City was on one of these family excursions. I remember going to the observation deck in the Empire State Building and being on a tour bus where someone pointed out men sleeping on the sidewalk as typical scenery in the Bowery. I remember dining at the Automat, where you chose from hot meals, cold salads, rolls, and desserts in individual little windows. You put change in the coin slots to open the window and extract what you had selected. They had nothing like this back home.

When I went off to college, I made friends with people from other parts of the country; we shared stories and dreams, and my horizons expanded. We used to hitchhike to other college towns or to the big city. To be stranded from time to time, alongside a highway, seemingly in the middle of nowhere—that was an experience to be relished.

In our own cars, we made road trips to all sorts of places. Once a friend and I tooled through the countryside for two or three days just to find things we had read about—like a particular beach or the world's largest chair in the square of a North Carolina furniture factory town. Those were great trips.

For a time I daydreamed about shipping out on a freighter to see the world. I'd leave the ship when I got someplace I really wanted to see and live there for a while. Who knows: someday I might return to America, wise beyond my years. I'd be an experienced world traveler. Ah, dreams.

I married a girl from out of town, so I had to travel to see her when we were courting. Fortunately, she liked the idea of traveling, too. When we got married, we went to Nassau, in the Bahamas, on our honeymoon. It was our first tropical island. Nassau was just as the travel brochures showed it—sparkling, clear water; white, powdery sand; blue sky and blazing sun. I got so sunburned by our third day there that I was walking like an old man. But what a time we had. We arrived home with just enough change in our pockets to call someone to come and pick us up at the airport.

A Travel Career

As much as I liked to travel, I didn't really connect it to my first job as a newspaper reporter. There were some brushes with wanderlust in those days—when I'd go aboard a foreign flagship to interview the captain for a feature story or encounter a story subject who had traveled extensively. Once I interviewed daredevil aviator Douglas "Wrong Way" Corrigan when he visited friends in my town. He was quite old. I barely knew of the air travel exploits in

1938 on which his renown was based, but Corrigan still told his story with a crackle to it.

After a couple years of newspapering, I got a job with a big-time magazine. We moved to a new and bigger city. I began traveling in my work. Finally I was able to combine my love of travel and my job. Often my wife went along as I gathered stories across the landscape. We loved it, and it was the start of my career as a travel writer and editor. Eventually I took a job as the travel editor for *Better Homes & Gardens* magazine in Des Moines, Iowa. That was in 1967. We've been traveling, and I've been writing about our travels, ever since. I also have written about jobs and careers over the years, primarily with *Kiplinger's Personal Finance Magazine* and with the Association for Career and Technical Education. So in this book, I have the opportunity to combine the two subjects.

Jobs for Travel Buffs

What you will find herein is information about more than a score of careers in which travel plays an important part. Although some of these career fields are small, with relatively few workers, all of them are open to anyone who will put in the time and effort to prepare for the field.

When we think travel careers, we tend to think first of jobs in transportation—with airlines, railroads, cruise lines, and shipping companies—and of travel agents. But as you will learn here, you don't have to be a pilot, railroad engineer, ship captain, or bus driver in order to travel in your work. There are several dozen kinds of jobs, for people with a variety of skills, in which travel is an important part of the work routine.

There are also some traveling jobs—such as those of high-powered politicians, diplomats, rock stars, and astronauts—that few people can hope to land. But who knows; if space exploration expands, thousands of travel buffs with every work skill known to society could be needed for great adventures in outer space.

In each chapter that follows, you will find a description of what a field is like and what kind of jobs it supports—including where travel fits into the routine. The outlook for job growth in a particular field is based on this U.S. Bureau of Labor Statistics scale: average job growth is 10 to 20 percent; faster than average is 21 to 35 percent; much faster than average is 36 percent or more; more slowly than average is 3 to 9 percent; little or no change is zero to 2 percent; decline is down 1 percent or more. If you're interested, you can read on to discover exactly how to get into that field, what typical pay scales are, the training and background you must have, and where you can get more detailed information about the career field and preparing for it. Unless otherwise noted, this information is applicable to workers in the United States and Canada; however, earnings figures are in U.S. dollars. Many of the information sources are international organizations. Where available, both website addresses and street addresses are listed.

For general information about the travel and tourism industry in the United States and Canada consult these sources:

Travel Industry Association of America
1100 New York Avenue NW, Suite 450
Washington, DC 20005
www.tia.org

Tourism Industry Association of Canada
1608 – 130 Albert
Ottawa, ON K1P 5G4
Canada
www.tiac-aitc.ca

CHAPTER ONE

Travel Agents, Tour Guides, and Tourism Promoters

Travel Agents

Nearly everyone who travels may eventually turn to a travel agent for help in planning a trip. Travel agents sell travel. They make recommendations about destinations to visit and how to get there. They also make transportation, hotel, and tour package reservations for you. After paying the bill, all you have to do is get to the airport or pier on time.

Of course, buying travel is a bit more complicated than buying a new pair of shoes, and it's a lot more expensive. The tab for a couple planning a two-week tour in Europe can be in the $5,000 to $15,000 range. With that kind of purchase, good travel agents pride themselves on giving their clients lots of information and helpful advice. Especially for international travel, there is much to know about—customs regulations, passports, visa requirements, certificates of vaccination, currency exchange, and rules of the road for drivers.

Travel-planning sites on the Internet let you select the elements of a trip and book air, hotel, and other reservations. For the simplest of trips this may do fine. But you may still need the savvy advice of a travel agent. Is the price you got on the website really the cheapest? Are there any hidden costs such as port charges or departure taxes? Your travel agent should know.

Promotion

Travel agents can't just wait for customers to walk in with their checkbooks in hand. Agents must know how to attract business and how to keep their clients coming back for pleasurable trips.

One way agents do this is by promoting their expert knowledge of the tourist destinations of the world and of the logistic and mechanical intricacies of travel. They have access to all sorts of published and computer-based sources of data on all elements of a trip—airline, train, and cruise line schedules and fares; availability of discounts; the range of hotel rates; package tour ingredients and prices; rental car deals; critical ratings of individual hotels and restaurants.

Travel agents also attend meetings of special-interest groups where they can give slide shows or other presentations about their services, and they regularly call on major firms to solicit their business travel accounts.

The Daily Routine

The way travel agents acquire much of their knowledge is by taking trips. Nothing beats firsthand experience and observations. Airlines, cruise lines, hotel chains, and tour operators regularly host travel agents on familiarization trips ("fam" tours) where agents can check out itineraries and facilities they'll sell to their clients.

Agents often go on fam tours in the off season at popular travel destinations. There is more space available then and more time for them to look around. Also, in the prime travel season, travel agents are usually chained to their desks and computer consoles working out travel plans for their customers.

Travel agents regularly visit hotels, resorts, and restaurants to rate firsthand their comfort and cleanliness and the quality of the food and wine. They base their recommendations on their own travel experiences as well as those of colleagues and longtime clients. Traveling is also a way to learn about typical weather conditions, off-the-beaten-path restaurants, sightseeing attractions, and recreation opportunities at destinations around the globe.

But even for travel agents, there is never enough time to travel. Most of their time is spent at their computer terminals and on phones conferring with clients and completing the paperwork that holds together a well-planned trip. Travel agents spend hours on the phone and computer—consulting with tour operators and guides, E-mailing clients and suppliers, and punching in data to track reservations and build client records.

Travel agents work everywhere. More than eight out of ten salaried agents work for travel agencies; others work for membership organizations with travel departments. Many travel agents are self-employed. Few towns are too small to support a travel agent. They work from offices in suburban areas, in large cities, and in small towns and rural areas.

Many agencies specialize—in business travel, cruises, adventure trips, personalized itineraries, or other niches. There are a number of major travel agencies that have hundreds of branch offices around the country and the world—American Express, Uniglobe, Carlson Wagonlit, and others.

Agencies that specialize in planning vacation trips are referred to as boutique agencies; they tend to be small and offer highly personalized service. Some agencies promote themselves as "discounters," giving back some of the commission to customers but offering little or no service other than ticket sales.

Independent agent Cindy Peters is a cruise specialist for Adventure Travels in Pompano Beach, Florida. "I started in this field by working for a large discount cruise agency," she says, "and after working there for four years and establishing a client base, I moved to a work environment where I basically run my own business within this agency.

"Since my clients are national instead of local, I have no 'walkin' business. I work by phone and E-mail. I typically work many hours a day, sometimes seven days a week, but don't mind at all because it is my own business. My clients call to get price quotes on specific cruises or land tours, and I get discounted rates for them on each trip. My motto has always been that I would not be undersold."

Peters says she loves working in the travel business and travels as often as she can get away. "Next month I will be sailing to Alaska with a large group of passengers in the almost one hundred cabins I booked. In the fall I will be trying out all the new cruise ships on a series of two-night sailings. Then over New Year's, I will take my family on a Disney cruise.

"It sounds like a lot of traveling, but I feel like the more ships I experience, the better salesperson I can be."

Getting into the Business

Becoming a travel agent requires specialized training. Technology and computers are having a profound effect on the work of travel agents. Computer skills are a basic requirement. Some employers want their agents to have college degrees in areas such as travel and tourism, computer science, geography, communications, accounting and business, world history, or foreign languages.

Few agencies train people on the job. They normally refer you to one of the many vocational schools that offer six- to twelve-week courses for beginning travel agents. Then, with actual work experience, plus further study and examinations over eighteen months, an agent can earn the coveted Certified Travel Counselor (CTC) designation from the Institute of Certified Travel Agents. Another mark of achievement in the field is a certificate of proficiency from the American Society of Travel Agents, which is awarded to agents who pass a three-hour exam.

A travel agent's job also requires the ability to work with computer databases and a head for basic business accounting and planning practices. Previous experience in the travel field is an asset. For example, some agents were previously airline reservations agents or ticketing agents.

An agent also needs good selling skills. Characteristics that help in this department are a pleasant personality, patience, and the ability to gain the confidence of clients. Agent-client trust is a key here. For potential clients, choosing a travel agent is like choosing a doctor or lawyer—once the agent's competence has been established, the choice often comes down to personal chemistry and trust. This is where the personality and integrity of an agent are major assets. Personal travel experience is also an asset for an agent, since firsthand knowledge about destinations can help influence a client's travel plans, and the ability to continually steer clients to places and experiences they enjoy brings repeat business to an agent.

If you work for a travel agency, the agency often has earned formal approvals from travel suppliers such as air and rail lines and rental car companies. Those approvals enable travel agents to draw commissions when they sell the products of those companies. To earn those approvals, an agency must demonstrate that it is financially and operationally sound and has been in business for a period of time. In several states, travel agents must also be licensed. The toughest aspect of becoming a self-employed travel agent, or opening a new agency, is operating successfully for long enough to win the approvals from key suppliers that allow you to earn commissions.

Your Future as a Travel Agent

Job opportunities for travel agents are expected to grow more slowly than average. The reasons are that many more travelers are making their trip arrangements on the Internet, airline commissions to travel agents are lower than ever, and the terrorist air attacks on America on September 11, 2001, depressed the travel market for some time.

However, professionals are projected to be the fastest-growing occupational group, and they spend significant amounts on business and leisure travel. Cruise lines rely heavily on agents to book trips on their ships. And despite the growth of Internet users, some people always will want an agent's help. So some job openings will be created as new travel agencies open and existing ones expand, but most growth will come as agents retire or otherwise leave the field and need to be replaced.

Spending on travel increases as business activity expands. Also, as incomes rise, more people travel on vacations and do so more frequently. Many people take more than one vacation a year. Airfare deals and larger, more efficient planes have brought air travel within the budgets of more people than ever before. So growing numbers of travelers will seek travel agents to help them arrange their trips.

A note of caution: The travel industry is very sensitive to economic conditions. When the economy slumps and people are pinched in the pocketbook, travel plans are the first things to be put off in order to get through the economic hard times. So travel agencies often find that the volume of their business fluctuates and is dependent on the state of the economy as a whole.

Earnings and Benefits

Earnings of travel agents depend largely on commissions from the sale of travel products. Those who are employees of agencies may draw base salaries and receive some fringe benefits. According to one survey, median annual earnings of travel agents are $25,150, including commissions. Overall agent salaries range from about $15,900 to $39,300, with managers of agencies earning more.

The commission rate for domestic travel purchases—such as cruises, air tickets, hotels, package tours, and car rentals—is about 7 to 10 percent of total sales; for international travel elements, it's about 10 percent. Sometimes travel agents are asked to put together special itineraries. This may involve coordinating various air and ground transportation connections, placing international calls to make reservations at exclusive hotels, and offering other extraordinary services or arrangements. Especially since some airlines have squeezed sales commissions, travel agents may charge a service fee on top of the commission for the extra time and cost involved in making these special arrangements.

Earnings of self-employed agents, of course, are totally dependent on commissions and service fees. When they are just starting out and don't yet have commission approval from airlines and car rental companies, self-employed agents must survive on commissions from suppliers who don't require formal approval. Such suppliers include cruise lines, hotels, and tour companies. Therefore, earnings for self-employed travel agents may be very low at the start.

As key sales agents for travel industry suppliers, travel agents usually get substantial discounts when they travel (up to 75 percent off the cost of transportation and accommodations). Sometimes they travel free as the guests of airlines, hotels, and destinations that want the agents to experience their services and products and recommend them to future clients.

For More Information

American Society of Travel Agents
1101 King Street
Alexandria, VA 22314
www.astanet.com

Association of Retail Travel Agents
2692 Richmond Road, Suite 202
Lexington, KY 40509
www.artaonline.com

Institute of Certified Travel Agents
148 Linden Street
Wellesley, MA 02482
www.icta.com

Tour Guides and Managers

Do you have a keen sense of history? Do you love to share your knowledge of the lore and legends of places with your friends and colleagues? Are you a good people person, able to mix with folks of all types and have them look to you for direction? Have you the unique ability to talk while walking backwards?

You do? Then you could be a tour guide.

Professional tour guides trace their craft to the eighteenth-century tradition of the European cicerone (after ancient Roman orator and philosopher Cicero). The cicerone was the local interpreter who explained the history and curiosities of a place to visitors. The wealthy citizens who could travel the world would seek appointments with the cicerone of a city or region to learn everything about it—its history, architecture, culture, commerce, and people. In this way, influential travelers from distant places came to better understand one another's societies. The efforts of ciceroni helped civilize the world; suspicions and other barriers between regions were lowered.

Today the cicerone is the professional tour guide. Actually, the profession includes several types of guides: tour managers, who escort and manage a group's travel on a multiday tour; tour guides, who take people on sight-seeing excursions of more limited duration; driver/guides, who both drive a tour motorcoach and provide narration en route, usually on local tours; step-on guides, or city guides, who come aboard a touring motorcoach to provide expert information about the city; and docents, usually volunteers, who lead tours of museums.

John Stavely, tour guide and trainer for "Tour Saint Augustine" in St. Augustine, Florida, came to the field with a background in theatre and public speaking and in the golf, restaurant, and hospitality businesses. He leads historic, "team-building," and entertainment tours from thirty minutes to multiple days in duration. He also trains guides in how to interpret and interact with their groups to enhance the experience.

"On a typical day," says Stavely, "I might greet a group of twenty school children at 9 A.M. and give them a one-hour tour of a historical site, such as our defensive fort, maybe followed by another student group at 10 A.M. After lunch, as a step-on guide, I might meet a corporate group of forty on a motorcoach and give them a two-hour tour of our town with several stops at historical sites for a look, interpretation, and picture taking. Then at 8 P.M., I'll lead a walking ghost tour of haunted locations for a senior church group. At 10 P.M., I'm done for the day. But I really enjoy my work," he says.

A dozen times a year he travels to visit other attractions, where he gets ideas for his own tours, and he attends industry meetings, such as the Meeting Professionals International conference or the Florida Attractions Association, to network, promote his company, and learn from others in the business.

Tour guiding can be a glamorous life, covering as many miles as you care to spend on the road each year. But those who make it their career find that life as a tour guide also has its frustrations and shortcomings.

The Work

Life as a traveling tour guide isn't a continuous carefree journey throughout the world. It is shepherding forty or so bus passengers around a town, state, or region of the world in all kinds of weather, tending to their various needs. Tour guides on multiday tours are on call twenty-four hours a day and must minister to passengers who need medical attention, have strayed from the group, get arrested by the local police, or have other problems that they expect the guide to at least help them solve. And to be successful, guides must perform these wonders with aplomb!

The occupation does offer many satisfactions. As a guide, you have the opportunity to meet people from all over the world. If you are a locally based guide, you become the official spokesperson and goodwill ambassador for a city, region, or the entire country to the travelers you serve. As the modern-day cicerone, you can help bridge cultural differences as you explain sights and sounds to visitors on tour.

Travelers on group tours look to guides as educators. They want to learn about the places they visit, and they expect you to have authoritative answers to all their questions. Travelers also expect you to educate them in an entertaining manner. Of course, guides learn from their charges, too. Many guides tell of regularly receiving letters from passengers who have taken their tours. Veteran travelers have been known to book only tours that their favorite guides will be leading.

"Working in the travel business is my passion and my profession," says Jo Curran, a tour guide for thirty-five years. She got into the field as a volunteer walking tour guide in York, England. She moved to Innsbruck, Austria, where she guided English-speaking tourists for pay. She later worked guiding German-speaking tourists around Europe, and eventually she made her home in Seattle, Washington, where she's an independent tour guide.

Her work for tour companies sometimes also includes coordinating the tour with the motorcoach driver, entertaining the passengers, even working out arrangements for them with hotels and restaurants.

"When tour groups arrive at the airport, I greet them and look after *all* their needs for the length of the tour," says Curran. "I must see that everything promised in the sales brochure is delivered—

telling the passengers about everything we see on the motorcoach trip.

"As an independent contractor, I may work sixteen hours a day and be on call for the other eight hours, seven days a week, for weeks on end. We also have months without work and without income," she says.

Guides must know about group dynamics in order to make sure each individual in a tour group is recognized in some way and is able to appreciate the trip and the guide's narrative. Of course, to survive in this field, a guide basically must like people. In addition, guides must be well educated, especially in history, geography, and civics. It helps if they have learned something about psychology, speech, and drama as well. Guides must base their narrative programs on solid research, including keeping up with current events in various locales. The most successful guides also possess specialized knowledge in certain subjects, such as art, architecture, archaeology, and the like. Those who are fluent in foreign languages can earn higher fees.

Crisis management is also a skill professional guides must acquire. As the leader of a group of people on the road, a guide has to be able to cope with emergencies and contingencies that can rattle the untrained—a driver who becomes incapacitated, a fire on a motorcoach, the illness or death of a passenger, foul-ups involving hotel reservations and other travel arrangements. Guides routinely have to deal with maps, itineraries, timetables, airline check-in procedures, and early morning bag pulls from hotel corridors. To run a route, they need to know about traffic patterns on tour routes, availability of motorcoach parking at various destinations, procedures for entering tourist attractions.

For a guide, it pays to have a good sense of humor, an outgoing personality, honesty and ethics, diplomacy and tact. Good health also is important—to avoid becoming physically run down by the pace of travel (on your feet for hours at a time, eating on the run, infrequent restroom stops). And here's where the facility to walk backwards while talking comes in! That's a situation most tour guides frequently find themselves in while leading their charges through yet another lavish garden or restored frontier fort. Guides also often find themselves riding backward—as they must stand at the front of the motorcoach and address travelers about sights that are ahead of passengers but behind the guide.

Getting into the Business

Many tour guides sort of back into the field. They may be experts on certain subjects who start as local guides to historical sites or who lead special agricultural tours or ecotourism trips. These guides move on to longer-range, over-the-road tours. Licenses are required of guides in about five cities, but, for the most part, there are no formal requirements for becoming a tour guide.

Although she started as a volunteer, veteran tour guide Jo Curran says, "Today someone who has not been through a tour guide school hardly has a chance of getting a start in the business."

Some tour companies and destination management organizations, such as tourist bureaus, provide training to persons they hire for guide work. In many cases, in return for this training, you may be required to sign an agreement that you won't work for another company for a certain period of time.

Tour companies—the major employers of tour guides—know that good tour managers can influence passengers' decisions about taking repeat trips with the same company. So they are reluctant to take a chance on rookie guides. Since tour managers and guides are the frontline employees in the group travel field, how well they perform may mean millions of dollars in sales gained—or lost—by tour companies.

As a practical matter, most guides are college graduates; many have graduate degrees. Indeed, some guides are former college professors—knowledgeable people used to lecturing who turn to this profession because of their love of travel. And while you could simply send your resume to tour companies, getting special training in tour guiding will give you a leg up in the field.

A number of community colleges and universities offer courses in tourism management and tour guiding. For the most part, these six- to eight-week courses are taught by practicing tour guides and managers who bring practical experience and their theoretical knowledge to students. Among the better programs in the country are those at West Los Angeles College, Miami-Dade Community College, and Denver University.

There are also proprietary trade schools that offer tour-guiding and tour-managing programs. Many of them promote their ability to place graduates in jobs. Because these schools usually charge much more than public colleges, you should analyze their programs with care and a healthy skepticism. There are unscrupulous operators in this business who charge big bucks for superficial—or even worse—programs of instruction.

Your Future as a Tour Guide

Group travel is a major segment of the travel business, and it is with this segment that tour guides and managers are associated. Employment prospects for guides should continue to expand in the years ahead.

The majority of professional guides—tour managers—are employed by group tour companies, such as Tauck, Maupintour, Globus Gateway, and American Express. The balance of the field are freelancers, although some of these are more accurately small-business operators who organize and guide their own specialty tours.

In many ways, tour guiding is akin to teaching, and guides who are able to work the maximum number of assignments through the year, which may consist of several touring seasons, can earn slightly less than the national average for teachers. Of course, freelance guides don't have the job security and benefits of teachers. They get no health insurance, pension plan contributions, sick leave, paid vacation time, or unemployment compensation. And the work of a guide or tour manager isn't a typical nine-to-five job. Tour managers are on duty twenty-four hours a day, often for weeks at a time. A workweek of eighty-five hours is not unusual for a tour manager.

Of course, many freelance guides like the fact that they can work as much or as little as they want to and that they can pick and choose assignments not necessarily for money, but for the enjoyment they figure they'll get from certain tours and particular itineraries. Also, gratuities are common in this field. While no guide can count on them, for popular guides, money from tips can be substantial over time.

The field, part of the broad service workers segment of the workforce, is expected to grow as fast as average. Pay scales for tour guides range typically from $11 to $25 an hour. At those pay rates, and considering the seasonal nature of group travel, a successful freelance tour guide/manager could expect to earn $19,000 to $23,000 a year. Tour managers employed by major tour companies will work more steadily and may enjoy valuable fringe benefits that freelancers don't have. These employed tour managers and guides may earn up to $60,000 or $65,000 a year, including gratuities.

The more credentials a guide has—such as college degrees and specialized courses and certificates—usually the higher the wage he or she will enjoy.

For More Information

International Association of Tour Managers
North American Region
9500 Rainier Avenue South, Unit 603
Seattle, WA 98118
http://members.aol.com/iatmone

National Association of Interpretation
P.O. Box 2246
Fort Collins, CO 80522
www.interpnet.com

International Guide Academy
P.O. Box 19649
Boulder, CO 80220
www.igaonline.com

Miami-Dade Community College
Hospitality and Tourism Management Program
  (or Travel Industry Management)
11380 Northwest Twenty-Seventh Avenue
Miami, FL 33167
www.mdcc.edu

West Los Angeles College
Department of Travel
9000 Overland Avenue
Culver City, CA 90230
www.wlac.cc.ca.us

Public Relations Professionals

Whenever a new hotel manager is appointed, a brief story about the executive and his or her position is distributed to the media in the form of a press release. Before the start of each season, press releases about rates and attractions at resorts and tourist destinations go out to hundreds of travel writers and editors. Cruise lines, tour companies, hotel chains, resorts, cities, and states all must keep the public aware of the delightful holiday and vacation opportunities they offer. These messages are cranked out continuously by cadres of public relations representatives who convey their information to the media in the hope that it will make the papers or the six o'clock news.

In order to produce media releases about the delights of Loews Miami Beach Hotel, a Carnival cruise, the beaches of the

Caribbean, the fun and frivolity of Southern California, the pleasures of an Italian rental villa, and the fjords of Alaska, public relations people must visit those destinations, check them out, and dig out facts and figures that they can pump into their releases to attract media attention.

Public relations specialists work for every kind of business and institution. But those employed by companies in the travel and hospitality industry generally travel the most and to glamorous locations.

On the Job

An organization's reputation and profitability—even its continued existence—may depend on how successfully it presents its goals, policies, plans, products, and successes to the world. Public relations representatives devise and execute plans to mold the right image for the business and its products and services.

Everybody needs public relations people—businesses, government agencies, individuals, schools and universities, public interest groups, trade associations. And whatever the nature of the client organization, the public relations job usually requires some travel. PR people may go on the road to do field research on client properties or to visit and build relationships with community and media representatives in areas where the client sells products and services.

Public relations involves not only telling an organization's story, but also understanding the attitudes and concerns of customers, employees, and the community at large and helping management formulate sound policies for dealing with those constituencies. Public relations representatives deal not only with the press and community groups, but also with government agencies and regulators, political officials, and businesses. They may also write speeches, accompany clients to media interviews and on public-speaking engagements, and deal deftly with inquiries from the press and public.

Some public relations people work directly for the business or institution they represent, such as a hotel chain or state tourism bureau. Others work for independent PR agencies that usually have client relationships with a number of different businesses. It's not unusual for a business to utilize the services of both its own in-house PR reps and an outside agency, especially when planning special events, for example. Most PR people work directly for institutions they represent; about 10 percent work for independent PR firms; another 10 percent are self-employed PR agents.

Independent public relations firms often specialize in certain kinds of clients. For example, some are well known for representing politicians or Hollywood stars and billionaires. Others specialize in handling the public images of specific kinds of businesses—banks and financial institutions, auto manufacturers, technology companies, or travel industry clients such as hotels, resorts, cruise lines, tour operators.

A veteran of in-house PR for three cruise lines, Kathleen Jane Dunlap now runs her own public relations company, Dunlap Consulting International, LLC, from Lexington, Virginia, a Shenandoah Valley college town.

"I like the lifestyle and flexibility of focus I have in running my own business," she says. "I can manage my own time and choose my clientele. I keep regular hours, nine to five, Monday through Friday. My time is occupied with working on proposals for clients, drafting PR plans, meeting with clients and media contacts, and traveling to conferences and client events."

Dunlap specializes in the travel field. Her clients include Society Expeditions, a high-brow, upscale cruise line that sails to Antarctica and other remote locales; the small Polynesian island nation of Niue; Nelson County in Virginia, an outdoor recreation destination; Shenandoah Shakespeare, a touring and teaching theater company; and Blackfriars Theater in Staunton, Virginia.

"Each client requires a different set of services," she says. "Most often I provide media relations services, but I also do strategic planning for companies, arrange and conduct press trips, write and edit materials, and handle special events. Sometimes I develop cooperative promotional partnerships for my clients.

"Years ago, I traveled three weeks out of a month for a stretch of years. Now I travel to places around the United States four or five times a year, internationally usually once, and make local day trips once a week or so.

"I love doing travel PR. There is a wonderfully positive community of professionals in the field, even in tough economic times. Cooperation is the name of the game in tourism. That is not the case in other industries where turf protection and fear of sharing knowledge or assistance more often than not rule working relationships."

Getting into the Business

Public relations has a long and colorful history. Its earliest days were marked by flackery, from which came the stereotype of the hustling, brassy publicity agent. As the field matured, however, its hard edges were smoothed. The profession became more polished; the techniques, more sophisticated; and the operating rules, more reputable.

Today's PR people usually are college graduates. They must deal with top officials and managers of client companies and institutions, so a university background is necessary. Indeed, many colleges and universities offer degree programs in public relations, usually as part of a communications or journalism curriculum.

PR people as a rule are cool, sophisticated, smooth handlers of public pronouncements and media inquiries. Look at how well the U.S. armed forces PR officers (usually called public information officers when they work for the military, government, or public institutions) handled the often-irritating inquiries of the press during the war on terrorism in Afghanistan.

As a PR person you don't have to be the ultimate expert on the business or product or service you are representing, but you should be able to quickly make yourself conversant on the basics of the subject. And you must know to whom you can refer the media for detailed, expert follow-up information. Of course, when you sit down to write a series of news releases, you should take the time to do the research that will give your writing deeper authority.

The ability to research and communicate well through various media is a requirement for success in the PR field. Another key aspect of the work is being able to conceptualize the goals and objectives of an overall PR strategy to communicate a client's message over time.

Qualifications for PR jobs include creativity, the ability to express your thoughts clearly and simply, good writing and public-speaking skills, and a lot of drive and initiative. It also helps to have an outgoing personality, self-confidence, some understanding of human psychology, and an enthusiasm for motivating people.

Mindy Bianca is an in-house public relations coordinator for her employer, the Maryland Office of Tourism Development. She began her career as a journalist, then turned to public relations when a publication she worked for foundered and she found her present job.

"I'm responsible for generating positive print and broadcast stories about Maryland destinations," says Bianca. To do that she coordinates visits to the state for travel journalists, attends conferences and expositions where she can meet journalists and encourage their interest in covering Maryland, and sends press releases about state attractions to hundreds of media contacts.

"There's really no such thing as a 'typical' workday," says Bianca, "and that's part of what I really like about this job. There's never a dull moment, and there's always something interesting waiting around the corner. I need to be out and about, and I thrive on interaction with others.

"On any given day, I might be escorting a press tour for an individual journalist or a group of seven writers from a foreign country; helping an author fact-check a guide book; planning a press conference about a new tourism site; appearing on a radio show to promote tourism in Maryland; attending a travel writers' or public relations professionals' conference to make media contacts and learn how to do my job better."

Bianca travels in state several times a week and out of state about once a month, usually for four to seven days, mostly for conferences or media expos. She often uses her "comp" time—overtime hours not compensated for—to stay an extra day or two at her own expense to explore the conference destinations.

"I've spent time in some fabulous places," says Bianca, "It's not just a way to relax and have a minivacation, but it's also a way to become a better travel professional. The more I know about other destinations, the better I can promote Maryland to travel journalists and our tourism partners.

"You'll never find nicer people than the ones in the tourism industry. There's a real sense of 'family' when you're what the folks around my office call a 'road warrior.' I feel that I have a friend in every major city or region of the world that I'd ever end up in."

Your Future in PR

In an increasingly competitive business environment, jobs for PR professionals are expected to grow at a much faster than average clip in the years ahead. Even smaller companies and institutions are likely to need the services of PR people.

Salaries in the field are comparable with those in other business services occupations. Annual earnings for PR reps range from $29,610 to $53,620, with the median about $39,580. The highest-paid 10 percent of those in the field make $70,480 or more a year. Superstars in this profession are in the megabucks category.

For More Information

Public Relations Society of America
33 Irving Place
New York, NY 10003
www.prsa.org

Society of American Travel Writers
1500 Sunday Drive, Suite 102
Raleigh, NC 27607
www.satw.org

Association of Travel Marketing Executives
20 North Avenue, Suite 4
Larchmont, NY 10538
www.atme.org

Travel & Tourism Research Association
P.O. Box 2133
Boise, ID 83701
www.ttra.com

International Association of Business Communicators
One Hallidie Plaza, Suite 600
San Francisco, CA 94102
www.iabc.com

Travel Writers and Other Journalists

Freelance Travel Writers and Photographers

Among the occupations most directly associated with the enjoyable side of travel is that of the travel writer and photographer. Often one person plays both roles—writing travel stories and also taking the pictures to illustrate them. There is no question that travel writers travel.

And when they travel, travel writers often get the red-carpet treatment—a bowl of fruit in the hotel room, a personal guided tour of prime tourist sites, lavish meals in the best restaurants. Hotels, bed-and-breakfast inns, restaurants, cruise lines, theme parks, tour companies, airlines, and vacation destinations want travel writers to report good things about them. So when travel writers come calling, travel suppliers put on their best faces.

Of course, the amount of special treatment travel writers receive usually depends on how much publicity they can offer in return. A visit by the travel writer whose articles appear in three or four small-town newspapers in the heartland of America may not cause the heartbeats of hoteliers, chefs, and destination promoters to race. But when someone like Rick Steves, guidebook author and host of popular TV travelogues, drops in, that's a different story. Travel suppliers pray for visits from influential journalists and go all out to assure that they gather good impressions to pass on to the thousands of people who read their articles and guides, watch their television shows, and attend their travelogue lectures.

On the Job

Visiting other places, be they around the globe or down the street, is, of course, a major part of being a travel writer. If freelance writers had to pay full price for every hotel room, airline ticket, attraction pass, or cruise cabin, they would never be able to travel to enough places to build the experience needed to advise readers and viewers about their best travel options. When a freelance writer needs to travel to far-flung destinations to gather story material, he or she can often get special help and discounts from travel suppliers—hotels and resorts, airlines and railroads, or destination convention and visitors bureaus. Like travel agents, travel writers also go on familiarization trips that are sponsored by these suppliers.

Many U.S. publications say this arrangement is a conflict of interest and refuse to buy travel stories from writers who accepted free or reduced-rate accommodations. But because few publications pay the travel expenses for freelance writers to get to a faraway destination to collect firsthand impressions and interviews, these discounts are a necessary evil.

Those who object usually feel that special treatment and discounts will obligate the travel writer to give favorable reviews to their hosts, but this is not necessarily the case. In fact, this practice is not unique to travel writers. Publishers give free books to reviewers; movie studios provide critics with tickets, the best seats in the house, and exclusive interviews with stars; professional sports teams provide front-row and box seats to sportswriters and broadcasters who cover the games; politicians let political reporters tag along on their bus tours. If writers and broadcasters are professionals with integrity, they'll tell their stories truthfully no matter how they managed to get where they needed to go to collect their story material.

Not every travel story requires travel. Travel writers need to know how the industry works. And that takes lots of research into airline fare structures, hotel operations, and the like. Travel writers don't write or broadcast reports only about tropical beaches, luxury hotels, and glamorous destinations; they must also tell their audiences how to get the best price deals on airline tickets and hotel rooms, how to protect themselves from pickpockets when on the road, where to find shopping bargains, how to avoid crowds at popular destinations, and lots of other information on the mechanics of travel.

Also, freelancers spend much of their time marketing their services to editors of newspapers, magazines, guidebooks, and other media. Many use the Internet to sell advice directly to travelers. Some sign up to give lecture tours. Travel photographers often work with photography stock houses, companies that store millions of images by thousands of photographers and market them worldwide to photo editors of all kinds of publications.

Your Future as a Freelance Travel Writer

As with every profession, there is a range of earnings to be found in travel writing. For the most part, relatively few freelancers regularly make sales at high rates to the top travel magazines, such as *National Geographic Traveler, Travel + Leisure,* and *Condé Nast Traveler.* It's more common for a writer to receive $50 or $100 per article.

For those freelancers who succeed in getting published, travel writing can be a great career. The travel industry is a global enterprise and a major business everywhere in the world. The economies of whole countries, such as the Bahamas and the principalities of Liechtenstein and Monaco, depend on tourism. Travel builds bridges of understanding among people throughout the world. Travel and tourism are important subjects and need to be covered in the media.

For More Information

Society of American Travel Writers
1500 Sunday Drive, Suite 102
Raleigh, NC 27607
www.satw.org

National Writers Union
National Office East
113 University Place, Sixth Floor
New York, NY 10003
www.nwu.org
   (Or look for union locals in your phone book.)

National Writers Union
National Office West
337 Seventeenth Street, #101
Oakland, CA 94612
www.nwu.org

American Society of Journalists and Authors
1501 Broadway, Suite 302
New York, NY 10036
www.asja.org

American Society of Media Photographers
150 North Second Street
Philadelphia, PA 19106
www.asmp.org

International Group of Speakers Bureaus
6845 Parkdale Place, Suite A
Indianapolis, IN 46254
www.igab.org

International Platform Association
101 North Center Street
Westminster, MD 21157
www.internationalplatform.com

Other Journalists

Travel is a way of life for many other writers, photographers, reporters, and correspondents for newspapers, magazines, radio, TV, and Internet media. They go wherever they must to pursue stories. Some accounts of how reporters tracked down a big story are as fantastic as the exploits of Indiana Jones in Steven Spielberg's series of adventure movies. The open-mike reporting by TV correspondents from Middle East sites in the war on terrorism seemed almost like a made-for-TV movie.

Reporters and correspondents for major news organizations—newspapers, magazines, broadcast and cable television networks, international news syndicates—gather information and prepare stories that inform their audiences about what's happening in their hometowns, the nation, and in villages, cities, and countries around the world. Media correspondents roam the globe to cover wars, celebrations, sports events, natural disasters, culture, and politics. They interview people, from men and women on the street to public officials, corporate executives, special-interest groups, kings and queens, rock stars, scoundrels, and cute children and animals. The world is their oyster.

A Reporter's Life

In covering a story, journalists investigate leads and news tips, pore through documents, interview people, and make observations on the scene. They organize the material they've gathered, decide on a focus or emphasis, and write their stories and video scripts to meet the deadlines of their papers, wire services, radio stations, or TV networks. Many of them write on portable laptop computers and send their word-processed stories by modem to their editors.

Video journalists usually work in tandem with a camera and sound crew on the scene of the story. Often they must compose the story on the fly without time to organize their notes. These dramatic reports from scenes of events, transmitted to our TV screens via satellite, can be memorable. If there is time, these journalists work with a video editor in a fixed or mobile studio to prepare a taped report with pictures and narration.

In the TV business, producers usually are the equivalent of newspaper reporters; they research and pull together information for live or taped video programs and reports. The "talent"—such as a network or station personality, news anchor, or special news correspondent—may actually appear on camera to deliver the producer's report.

Large newspapers, broadcasting stations, and TV networks assign reporters to specific "beats"—either geographic locations, areas of interest, or specialized fields. A journalist's beat might be police, courts, military, the White House, Congress, state legislatures, health, politics, foreign affairs, sports, fashion, art, education, or business. Many news and information organizations station correspondents in major U.S. cities and in foreign countries to cover events occurring in these locations.

Reporters on small newspapers may cover all aspects of the local scene and also take photos, write headlines, lay out pages, edit wire-service copy, and write editorials. On some small weeklies, they may even have to sell subscriptions, solicit advertisements, and perform general office work.

In every medium, editors do some writing and, almost always, much rewriting and editing of the work of reporters and correspondents. Often their primary duties are to plan the content of books, magazines, newspapers, or news broadcasts and to supervise all preparation. Editors have a lot of say in what will appeal to readers and viewers, and they assign topics and events for reporters to cover.

Working conditions for journalists vary depending on where they work and what news medium they work for. Some work in comfortable, private offices; others work in personal workstations; some work in noisy rooms filled with the sound of clacking keyboards and voices of other writers on phones tracking down information. When reporting from the scene, radio and television reporters often have to work despite the distraction of curious onlookers, police, and other emergency workers. Of course, conditions on-site when covering wars, political uprisings, fires, floods, and such can be downright dangerous.

For journalists on almost any beat, the search for firsthand information can require travel. A journalist may visit diverse workplaces, from factories and mines to offices and laboratories, theaters and ballparks. Sports writers follow the teams they report on around the country. They may accompany the players on planes and buses in their journeys to stadiums and playing fields for away games.

Getting into the Business

About half of all reporters and correspondents work for newspapers, 30 percent work for radio and TV organizations, and the rest toil for magazines and wire services and as freelancers. A substantial number of writers and editors work on magazines and newsletters published by business and nonprofit organizations, such as professional and trade associations, labor unions, and religious organizations.

Most employers prefer to hire college graduates with degrees in journalism, English, or communications. They may also look for job candidates with experience on school newspapers or broadcasting stations or as interns with news organizations. For jobs at some major newspapers and radio and TV stations, an educational background in subjects related to specific beats, such as economics, political science, or business, can help you get the job. Fluency in a foreign language might be necessary for assignment to an overseas bureau.

All writers and editors must be able to express ideas clearly and logically. Creativity, intellectual curiosity (a "nose for news"), a broad range of knowledge, initiative, and persistence are valuable characteristics. You'll also need the ability to concentrate amid confusion and to produce under pressure. Other assets are poise and resourcefulness, a good memory, physical stamina, and emotional stability—to deal with pressing deadlines, irregular hours, and sometimes dangerous assignments. Journalists may have to work in unfamiliar places and must be adaptable and feel at ease with a variety of people.

It should go without saying that reporters and writers need good typing or word-processing skills. Some knowledge of photography is often a plus. Many entry-level positions are combination reporter/camera operator or reporter/photographer jobs. Those who pursue careers in TV journalism should feel at ease in front of a camera and microphone.

Most beginners start out with small publications or television stations. To join a larger paper or TV network usually requires several years of reporting experience. Only a few make it to the major city papers, national magazines, and TV network shows.

In small operations, beginning writers and editors may do a little bit of everything—from reporting and writing to editing video and news pages. Advancement may come only by moving to a bigger paper or station. In larger organizations, jobs usually are structured more formally. Beginners generally do research, fact checking, and copyediting. Eventually they take on full-scale writing or editing duties. Advancement comes as they are assigned more important articles to write or edit.

The job of journalist will afford you an opportunity for self-expression, but more important is your ability to present facts as objectively and succinctly as possible. Accuracy also is vital because, among other things, untrue or libelous statements can lead to costly lawsuits and the loss of your job.

Your Future as a Journalist

Because of many closings and mergers of newspapers, decreases in newspaper circulation and print and television advertising sales, employment of reporters and correspondents is expected to grow more slowly than average through the rest of the decade. Areas that promise some growth are radio and television, new publications in niche markets, and online media such as websites and online newsletters.

The need to replace reporters who leave the field will create most job openings. There is a lot of turnover in this occupation; many find the work and lifestyle too stressful and hectic, and they transfer to other occupations where their skills are valuable, especially public relations and advertising work.

Competition can be intense for reporting jobs on major metropolitan newspapers, TV networks, and national magazines. Most beginning journalists start out with publications and TV outlets in suburban areas and small towns. Talented reporters and writers who can handle highly specialized scientific or technical subjects will be at an advantage in the job market.

Demand for technical writers is expected to increase because of the continuing expansion of scientific and technical information and the need to communicate it. The competition for technical writing jobs may not be as keen as for other areas of the writing business because of the more limited number of writers who can, and want to, work with technical material.

Yearly salaries for reporters working for daily newspapers range from about $16,540 to $69,300 and more. The median is $29,110. The highest-paid 10 percent in the field earn about $69,300 or more. Senior editors on large-circulation newspapers and magazines average over $60,000 per year.

The median salary of radio and TV reporters is $33,550. A National Association of Broadcasters/Broadcast Cable Financial Management Association survey shows that weekday local TV anchors earn $83,400 on average. Weekend anchors are paid an average of $44,200; sportscasters, about $68,900; weather reporters, $68,500. Radio newscasters and sportscasters earn about $12,000 a year less than their TV counterparts.

For More Information

National Newspaper Association
P.O. Box 7540
Columbia, MO 65205
www.nna.org

National Newspaper Publishers Association
3200 Thirteenth Street NW
Washington, DC 20010
www.nnpa.org

American Society of Magazine Editors
919 Third Avenue, Twenty-Second Floor
New York, NY 10022
www.asme.magazine.org

National Press Photographers Association
3200 Croasdaile Drive, Suite 306
Durham, NC 27713
www.nppa.org

Association for Education in Journalism and Mass
    Communication
University of South Carolina
234 Outlet Pointe Boulevard
Columbia, SC 29210
www.aejmc.org

The Newspaper Guild
Research and Information Department
501 Third Street NW, Suite 250
Washington, DC 20001
www.newsguild.org

National Association of Broadcasters
Career Center
1771 N Street NW
Washington, DC 20036
www.nab.org

Radio & Television News Directors Association
1600 K Street NW, Suite 700
Washington, DC 20006
www.rtnda.org

National Association of Broadcast Employees & Technicians
  Communications Workers of America International
  NABET/CWA
501 Third Street NW
Washington, DC 20001
www.nabetcwa.org

CHAPTER THREE

Airline and Ship Crews

Airline Pilots

Airplane pilots are highly trained, skilled professionals. They can qualify to fly many kinds of fixed-wing aircraft and helicopters. And they fly these craft on a variety of missions.

Most of us who travel are familiar with the role of passenger-airplane pilots. We hear from them every time we fly, usually at the beginning and end of a flight to announce seat belt and other safety and security regulations in preparation for take-off and landing. On some small commuter and corporate planes, you are in closer contact with the pilots; they may even supervise the seating of passengers and the stowing of luggage in order to balance weight in the aircraft.

But there are a lot of pilots we rarely see at work. For example, pilots of cargo planes fly freight to destinations all over the world. Those who pilot the big jets for the overnight delivery services—such as Federal Express, UPS, and Airborne—crisscross the world on regular schedules. Other pilots fly aircraft for aerial photographers, as test pilots for aircraft manufacturers, or with forest fire-fighting crews. Some pilots work for the airlines as examiners or check pilots. They periodically fly copilot to check on the proficiency of each pilot in the airline's employ.

Helicopter pilots are often involved in police work, supplying offshore oil platforms, land and sea rescue efforts, and major construction projects. They also transport passengers, often on sightseeing tours and for TV news shows.

About nine out of ten salaried civilian pilots work for commercial airlines; others work as flight instructors at local airports; some work for corporations that use their own aircraft to fly company cargo and executives.

As they move up in seniority, airline pilots may opt for choice international routes or prime cross-country flights in the United States. While this enables them to spend layovers of a day of two in far-flung cities of the world and premier tourist destinations, they are away from their homes and families much of the time.

The Life of a Pilot

On most airplanes, two pilots usually make up the cockpit crew. The captain, generally the more experienced pilot, is in command and supervises all other crew members. The copilot, or first officer, assists in communicating with air traffic controllers, monitoring the aircraft instruments, and flying the plane.

On larger airplanes on long international routes, there may be a third pilot on the flight deck—the flight engineer, or second officer, who assists the other pilots by monitoring and operating many of the on-board instruments and systems, making minor in-flight repairs, and watching for other aircraft. Current technology includes computerized controls and extensive video displays, which greatly assist pilots in getting the aircraft from destination to destination routinely.

Because they have the help of large support staffs on the ground, airline pilots perform few nonflying duties; there are some, however. Before and after each flight, pilots do record-keeping paperwork for the airline and the Federal Aviation Administration (FAA), which licenses pilots to fly, sets standards for job requirements such as medical exams, and otherwise monitors pilots' careers.

Pilots who fly corporate aircraft may have many more nonflying duties in their job descriptions. They routinely supervise the fueling of the aircraft, check passengers aboard, load baggage, and keep records on their flights and aircraft. In some cases, the pilot and copilot also attend to the needs of their executive passengers in flight, although on larger corporate planes there may be at least one flight attendant to deal with the passengers. Pilots who fly corporate airplanes might also find themselves scheduling flights, arranging for major maintenance, and even performing minor maintenance and repair work on their planes.

By federal law, airline pilots aren't allowed to fly more than 100 hours a month or more than 1,000 hours a year. Most airline pilots fly an average of 80 hours a month and work an additional 120 hours a month on nonflying duties.

Airlines operate flights at all hours of the day and night, so pilots' work schedules can be irregular. Based on seniority with the airline, pilots usually can choose particular flight routes and work patterns they prefer. Many of their flights require layovers away from home. The airline covers the costs of hotel accommodations, meals, ground transportation, and other layover expenses.

Pilots who are employed outside of the airline industry often have irregular schedules. They may fly thirty hours one month and ninety hours the next. And because they frequently have many nonflying duties, they sometimes have less time off work than airline pilots do. Except for corporate pilots, most pilots who work outside the airline industry don't encounter layovers in distant cities or even roam that far from home base in their flights. Their flying may be on a single short route, such as ferrying supplies and workers to offshore oil platforms or to construction sites.

Although flying does not require that much physical effort, the mental stress of being responsible for the safe flight of an airplane full of passengers, in all kinds of weather, can be taxing. The most stressful time for pilots is during takeoffs and landings, when they must be super alert and quick to react if something goes wrong. And, especially on international routes, pilots often suffer jet lag—disorientation and fatigue caused by many hours of flying through different time zones.

Getting into the Business

All pilots who are paid to transport passengers or cargo must have an FAA-issued commercial pilot's license with an instrument rating. Helicopter pilots must hold a commercial pilot's certificate with a helicopter rating.

Qualifying for these licenses takes some preparation. First, applicants must be at least eighteen years old and have 250 hours or more of flying experience. They must pass a rigorous physical examination, have 20/20 vision, good hearing, and no physical handicaps that could impair their performance as pilots. Applicants must also pass drug screening tests and a written test on the principles of safe flight, navigation techniques, and FAA regulations. Finally, they must demonstrate to FAA examiners their ability to pilot an airplane.

To be rated for instrument flying—in order to fly at night and in bad weather—pilot's license applicants must have a total of 105 hours of flight experience, including 40 hours flying by instruments. They must also pass a written exam on instrument flying procedures and regulations and demonstrate their ability to fly by instruments.

Licensed pilots who join an airline, especially at the entry level, usually must also pass written and in-flight examinations and security checks to earn a flight engineer's license.

To become a captain, a pilot must have an airline transport pilot's license. Applicants for this license must be at least twenty-three years old and have a minimum of fifteen hundred hours of flight experience, including night and instrument flying.

All these licenses are valid as long as a pilot can pass the periodic physical examinations and tests of flying skills required by FAA and airline company regulations.

Flight Schools

So how do you begin? Where do you learn to fly? You do it in military or civilian flight schools. The FAA certifies about six hundred civilian flying schools, including some at colleges and universities that offer degree credit for pilot training. Novice pilots usually learn to fly on a small, single-engine, fixed-wing airplane. As they gain skill and experience, they move to training on twin-engine craft and jets. Pilots trained in the military usually get substantial experience on jet aircraft and on helicopters, and this is highly valued by airlines and many businesses.

Most airlines require their pilots to have at least two years of college, but they prefer four-year college graduates. In fact, most pilots entering the commercial field have college degrees.

Because pilots must be able to make quick and accurate decisions under pressure, airlines reject applicants who do not pass required psychological and aptitude tests. Yet, depending on the supply of capable pilots in the job market, airlines may loosen their educational requirements and even their 20/20 vision requirement, allowing vision corrected to 20/20, for instance.

New airline pilots usually start as flight engineers. When they join the airline, they receive several weeks of intensive training in flight simulators and classrooms before being assigned to a scheduled flight. Of course, once they are working for the airline, pilots regularly receive additional training to keep them abreast of technological advances, such as wind-shear detection equipment, and of developments in security regulations.

Career advancement for pilots generally consists of moving up to other flying jobs. For example, a lot of would-be airline pilots start out as flight instructors for small flight schools, where they build up their flying hours while they earn money teaching. As they become more experienced, they occasionally fly charter planes or take on flying jobs with small air transport firms—like an air taxi company.

Then some of these pilots will advance to a corporate pilot's job or get a flight engineer's job with an airline. Once with an airline, advancement usually depends on the seniority provisions of pilots' union contracts. Typically, after two to seven years, flight engineers can advance, according to seniority, to copilot. Five to fifteen years after that, they can advance again to the position of captain. A pilot who doesn't work for an airline may advance to chief pilot in charge of aircraft scheduling in a large corporate flight setup or to manager of aircraft maintenance and flight procedures.

Your Future in the Sky

The job outlook for pilots should be favorable in the years ahead, with employment increasing at an average pace. However, employment of business pilots will grow more slowly than in the past. The military, which has been a major source of pilots for the commercial airlines, increased its benefits and financial incentives in an effort to retain more of its well-trained pilots. So the military is expected to be a diminishing source of new airline pilots. College graduates who have experience piloting jet aircraft and who hold commercial pilot's or flight engineer's licenses should have reasonably good job prospects in the airline industry.

Despite the 2001 terrorist attacks on America, which put the brakes on air travel for a time, both airline passenger and cargo traffic are expected to grow as population and income increase through the rest of the decade. At the same time, continuing computerization of flight management systems in new aircraft will continue to eliminate the need for flight engineers on those planes, which will restrict employment growth in that area. Also, downsizing of middle management jobs by businesses and increasing use of electronic communications media to do business could affect business travel and, subsequently, demand for new pilots. Job growth for pilots will come mostly through the need to replace pilots who retire or otherwise leave the field.

Airline pilots are highly paid. Salaries for commercial airline pilots, copilots, and flight engineers range from $36,000 to $145,000 or more. The median salary for this group is $110,940. Some senior captains of the largest aircraft can earn better than $165,000 a year. Earnings depend on a variety of factors, such as the type, size, and maximum speed of the plane and the number of hours and miles flown. Night and international flights sometimes bring a pilot extra pay. Pilots earn more flying jets than prop planes.

Pilots who work outside the airline industry don't make as much. Average salaries for these pilots range from about $24,290 to $92,000. The median is $43,300. The higher salaries usually go to pilots who fly jet aircraft.

Most U.S. and Canadian airline pilots are members of the Air Line Pilots Association, International (AFL-CIO). A handful of flight engineers are members of the Flight Engineers' International Association. Pilots employed by one airline belong to the Allied Pilots Association. A popular fringe benefit for pilots is that members of their families can fly free or at greatly reduced fares on their own and other airlines.

For More Information

Air Line Pilots Association, International
535 Herndon Parkway
Herndon, VA 20170
www.alpa.org

Air Transport Association of America
1301 Pennsylvania Avenue NW, Suite 1100
Washington, DC 20004
www.air-transport.org

For a list of FAA-approved flight schools, request a copy of the "List of Certificated Pilot Schools" from:

Superintendent of Documents
U.S. Government Printing Office
Washington, DC 20402

....

Flight Attendants

Is there any more glamorous figure in the lore of travel than the
flight attendant? A perfectly groomed, trimly curvaceous, flaxen-
haired girl with a perpetual smile, just waiting to bring you a drink
or a meal or a pillow or a magazine. That's the high-in-the-sky
fantasy image.

In reality, flight attendants are women and men who serve
aboard passenger airplanes to look after your safety and comfort
during a flight. They generally are well-groomed, just as any workers who deal directly with the public should be, but they aren't all
smiles, all blond, or all women. And they come in various shapes
and sizes (although some airlines still are hard-nosed about
weight standards for their passenger cabin crew members).

Indeed, the routine of the flight attendant can be a decidedly
unglamorous life at times—comparable to the job of a waitress or
bartender. Nevertheless, flight attendants do travel. Many of them
make the most of it, particularly those who are young and carefree. It's a thrill to be able to hop a flight to the opposite coast for
a weekend or take your layovers in some of the most exciting cities
in the world.

The Daily Routine

At least an hour before each flight, attendants are briefed by the
airplane's captain on such things as expected weather conditions
for the flight and any particular passenger problems. The attendants check to see that the passenger cabin is in order, that
supplies of food, beverages, blankets, and reading material are

adequate, and that first-aid kits and other emergency equipment are aboard and in working order. As passengers board the plane, attendants greet them, help them get settled, store their coats and carry-on luggage, or find pillows.

Then it's time for the routine that is so familiar to anyone who has flown even a few times on scheduled airlines. Before takeoff, the flight attendants remind passengers about the use of emergency equipment—seat cushion is a flotation device, lights along the floor lead to emergency exits, oxygen masks drop down automatically if needed.

Then the attendants check to see that all passengers have their seat belts fastened and seat backs upright. Lead, or first, flight attendants oversee the work of the other attendants while performing most of the same duties themselves.

Assisting passengers in the event of an emergency is the most important function of attendants. This may range from reassuring nervous passengers during bumpy encounters with strong turbulence to administering first aid to passengers who become ill to opening emergency exits and releasing evacuation chutes following an emergency landing. Flight attendants have been heroic in real emergencies and crashes. Some have lost their lives while trying to help passengers in these circumstances.

In the air, the routine is busy. The attendants deal with passengers' questions and special needs, help make small children and elderly and handicapped persons comfortable, serve drinks and snacks, and, after this routine, collect all those rumpled napkins, empty cups, cans, and other trash.

After the plane has landed and they have bid their passengers farewell, the flight attendants prepare reports on any medication given to passengers, lost and found articles, and the condition of cabin equipment. If this is a connecting stop, the flight attendants may have to tidy up the cabin before the next group of passengers boards the aircraft.

Since airlines operate around the clock, some attendants work at night and on holidays and weekends. They usually fly seventy-five to eighty-five hours a month and often spend an additional seventy-five to eighty-five hours a month on the ground preparing planes for flight, writing reports following completed flights, and waiting for planes that arrive late.

Because of variations in scheduling and limitations on flying time, many attendants have eleven or twelve days, or more, off each month. They may spend the night away from their home base about one-third of this time. As they do for pilots, the airlines cover the cost of hotel accommodations, meals, ground transportation, and incidental expenses during layovers.

With their blocks of time off and the benefit of free flights on a standby basis for themselves and immediate family members, flight attendants can vacation in destinations they don't get to visit on the job.

If the free travel seems like a super fringe benefit, don't forget that the flight attendants earn it. Their work can be strenuous and trying. Short flights require speedy cabin service. A rough flight can make serving drinks and snacks difficult—even dangerous. Attendants stand during much of the flight and must try to be pleasant and helpful no matter how tired they are or how demanding passengers may be.

Many flight attendants enjoy their jobs despite the hard work involved. Judy Schulte of Miami, Florida, spent her entire career as a flight attendant with Eastern Airlines. As a senior attendant, she opted for international and cross-country U.S. flights and traveled regularly to London, San Francisco, Las Vegas, New Orleans, and throughout the Caribbean.

Schulte has fond memories of some wonderful episodes in the air—like the time a live kangaroo in a suit (his handler was accompanying him to a promotional event) slipped out of his seat and bounded down the airplane aisle. And then there were the flights to Las Vegas: "For some reason, people would always ask,

'What time does the midnight show start?' I thought that was rather odd, so I would say eleven o'clock, and they would never bat an eye.

"I was there in the 1960s and 1970s, during the best years in the aviation industry," she recalls. "The airline was like family."

Getting into the Business

Most attendants work for commercial airlines, and most are stationed in major cities where the airlines have hubs or home bases. A small number of flight attendants work for large companies that operate their own corporate aircraft for business executives.

The airlines like to hire poised, tactful, and resourceful people who can deal comfortably with strangers. They must be in excellent health with good vision and the ability to speak clearly. Applicants usually must be at least nineteen to twenty-one years old, but some airlines have higher minimum age requirements.

Applicants must be high school graduates; those who have completed at least several years of college or have experience in dealing with the public are preferred. Flight attendants for international airlines usually are required to speak an appropriate foreign language fluently.

The major airlines usually require that newly hired flight attendants complete four to six weeks of intensive training in the airlines' own schools. Airlines that do not operate their own schools generally send their trainees to the school of a cooperating airline.

At these schools, the new attendants learn emergency procedures, such as evacuating passengers from an airplane, operating an oxygen system, and giving first aid. Attendants are taught flight regulations and duties, company operations and policies, and how to deal with terrorism. Those who work on international routes get additional training in passport and customs regulations. After they graduate from the airline school, attendants annually take twelve to fourteen hours of training in emergency procedures and passenger relations.

When they first go from training school to the field, attendants are assigned to one of the airline's bases. The new attendants are placed on "reserve" status, from which they are called to staff extra flights or fill in for attendants who are sick or on vacation. Reserve attendants on duty must be available on short notice.

Attendants usually remain on reserve status for at least a year; with some airlines, at some bases, it may take five years or longer to advance from reserve status. Once attendants move off the reserve list, they bid for regular base and flight assignments. Because assignment choices are based on seniority, usually only the most experienced attendants get the first choice of base and flights.

Eventually some longtime attendants transfer to positions as flight service instructors, customer service directors, recruiting representatives, or other administrative jobs.

Your Future as a Flight Attendant

Employment of flight attendants should grow at an average pace, sensitive to economic swings. Growth in population and income will boost the airline business. And with larger planes in the air, demand for attendants will increase (the Federal Aviation Administration requires one flight attendant for every fifty seats on an airplane).

On the other hand, expect keen competition for flight attendant jobs through the rest of this decade, as the number of applicants will greatly exceed the number of job openings. Those with at least two years of college and experience in dealing with the public have the best chance of being hired.

Why the competition for attendant jobs when the number of jobs will be increasing? It has to do with the image of the job. Despite the fact that airline travel today has lost some of the glamour of its earlier days, the airline industry is still considered an attractive field by many new workers. After all, think of the travel involved, the chance to see more of America and the world than most people ever will. And the opportunity for free travel for airline employees and their families is an attractive fringe benefit.

Also, as more career-minded people enter this field, job turnover will decline. Even so, most job openings for flight attendants are expected to result from the need to replace attendants who retire or transfer to other occupations. During economic slowdowns, when the demand for air travel declines, many flight attendants are put on part-time status or laid off. Until business picks up again for the airlines, few new attendants are hired.

According to the Association of Flight Attendants, earnings in this field range from a low of $18,090 to $83,630 for the highest-paid 10 percent of flight attendants. The median salary is $38,820. Flight attendants receive extra compensation for overtime work and for night and international flights, and they are paid a per diem for meals while on duty away from home. They are required to buy uniforms and wear them on the job. Uniform replacement items are usually paid for by the airlines, which also generally provide a small allowance to cover cleaning and upkeep.

Most flight attendants are members of the Association of Flight Attendants. Others belong to the Transport Workers Union of America, the Teamsters, or other unions.

For More Information

Association of Flight Attendants
1275 K Street NW, Fifth Floor
Washington, DC 20005
www.afanet.org

Transport Workers Union of America
80 West End Avenue
New York, NY 10023
www.twu.com

Other Airline Employees

Becoming a pilot or flight attendant isn't the only way for a travel buff to find a place in the airline industry. Most airlines offer their employees the opportunity to fly free, on standby status, or at reduced rates with reservations anywhere on the airline's route. When they are off duty, reservation clerks, aircraft mechanics, baggage handlers, and other employees who work at airline sales and administrative offices are eligible for this fringe benefit—as are members of their immediate families.

For More Information

Air Line Employees Association, International
6500 Sixty-Fifth Street, Suite 201
Chicago, IL 60638

Air Transport Association of America
1301 Pennsylvania Avenue NW, Suite 1100
Washington, DC 20004
www.air-transport.org

Cruise Ship Crews

Cruise ships are like small towns on the water—they have everything that you would find on Main Street, from dry cleaners to salons to nightclubs. So the range of jobs on these ships is almost as large as what exists on dry land. In addition to the waiters and cabin stewards that first come to mind, cruise ships need doctors, ministers, deejays, lifeguards, and manicurists, to name a few. But let's take a look at some of the more typical job opportunities on a ship.

Cruise ships have a marine crew—as on merchant ships—of deck and engineering officers and seamen and oilers. The officers usually hail from the country on which the ship's cultural atmosphere is based—Norway, Greece, Italy, Britain.

Cruise ships also have what is called a hotel staff. These crew members include the purser (like a hotel front office manager), the cruise director (the social and public relations manager), and managers of cabin and dining room services. These managers work hard to direct a large staff of deck and cabin stewards, dining-room captains, waiters, bartenders, activity directors (who coordinate fitness classes, bingo games, lectures), and entertainers (who perform in clubroom shows and may double as activity directors during the day).

There certainly are benefits to working on a cruise ship. You are surrounded by beautiful, often exotic, scenery and are contributing to a memorable (and perhaps once-in-a-lifetime) experience for the guests on board.

Hotel staff and marine crews usually get shore time when the cruise ship is in port, and those ports are usually delightful places to spend some recreational time. You will have to make the most of this time, as cruise ships are rarely in port for more than twelve hours.

However, as a young nightclub lighting man on a Caribbean cruise ship once said: "The pay's not great. The scene on the ship isn't idyllic. But there is this climate and having days off in some great places."

Jobs for cruise ship hotel staff persons are expected to grow as fast as average. Ask travel agents and major cruise lines, such as Carnival, Norwegian, Royal Caribbean, and Princess, for leads to companies that hire cruise ship hotel staff employees. Most of these companies are located in Miami, Los Angeles, and Seattle, from which cruise ships regularly sail.

Because most cruise ships are registered in foreign countries, even though the lion's share of them serve U.S. ports, pay scales for workers on these ships are not tracked by the U.S. government.

For More Information

Cruise Lines International Association
500 Fifth Avenue, Suite 1407
New York, NY 10110
www.cruising.org

The Merchant Marine

For a lot of young people with active imaginations, shipping out on a merchant ship to see the world ranks right up there with joining the circus or the navy. Just imagine. You'll get to see the world—at least the world's port cities! As a crew member on a deep-sea merchant ship, you'll build muscles handling equipment around the decks. You'll hear sea tales from the old hands that will make you wise beyond your years.

But joining the merchant marine is not quite like stories you may have read in adventure books or seen in films. The reality is that today's superships are goliaths whose momentum may carry them several miles forward after an "all stop" command. Paper charts, brass-framed compasses, and sextants—while still found aboard ships—have largely given way to computerized instruments that set courses and assist with steering and engine operation.

A typical seagoing merchant ship has a captain; three deck officers, or mates; a chief engineer and three assistant engineers; plus six or more deckhands and oilers. Larger vessels also have a full-time cook and helper.

The captain is master of this seagoing domain and supervises the operation of the ship and the work of the other officers and the crew. The captain is responsible for overseeing the loading and unloading of cargo or passengers, maintaining logs and other records of the ship's movements and cargo carried, and ensuring that proper procedures and safety practices are being followed at all times and that the machinery and equipment are in good working order.

Like a top boss ashore, the captain sets policy (in this case, course and speed) and designates assistants to carry out the functions necessary to achieve it.

The Work

Various members of the ship's crew steer the ship, operate the engines, signal to other vessels, and maneuver to avoid hazards and other ships. They determine the ship's position using navigation aids, celestial observations, and charts. They moor or dock the vessel in port.

On large vessels, captains are assisted by deck officers or mates. There might be a chief, or first mate, and second and third mates. They "stand watch" (oversee operation of the vessel) for specified periods, usually four hours on and eight off. On small ships, there may be only one mate, called a pilot on some inland vessels, who alternates watches with the captain.

Engineers (officially called marine engineers) operate, maintain, and repair propulsion engines, boilers, generators, pumps, and other machinery on a ship. There are usually four engineering officers—a chief engineer and first, second, and third assistant engineers—who stand watches in the engine compartments, overseeing operation of engines and machinery.

Deckhands help navigate and steer the ship, operate deck equipment, and keep the nonengineering areas in good condition. They look out for other vessels, obstructions in the ship's path, and aids to navigation—such as buoys and lighthouses (now mostly electronic beacons). At sea there are constant maintenance chores, such as repairing hawsers (lines), chipping rust, and painting and cleaning decks and other areas. Deckhands also maintain and operate deck equipment—lifeboats, anchors, winches, cranes, and other cargo-handling gear.

When the ship is docking or departing, the deckhands secure or release the lines that hold the ship to the dock. They also work at loading and unloading cargo. On larger ships, a boatswain or head seaman directs the work of the deckhands.

In the ship's engine rooms, marine oilers are the equivalent of deckhands topside. The oilers lubricate gears, shafts, bearings, and other moving parts of engines and motors. They monitor gauges and record data as they repair and adjust machinery.

Life at Sea

The life of a sailor is one that requires absence from home and family for extended periods. Ships might ferry cargo back and forth between several major ports, hauling crude oil between the Middle East and the United States or Japan, for instance. Or, ships may be assigned itineraries that have them dropping off and picking up cargo at a series of ports, often far-flung. At the end of a voyage, a ship may have circled the globe.

For long spells at sea, sailors may earn shore leaves. They might work thirty to ninety straight days and then have thirty or sixty days off. But some ships grant no shore leave.

Merchant marine officers and seamen, experienced and beginners, are hired through union hiring halls where representatives deal with shipping companies that control the ships. Generally the more seniority you have, the longer the voyage you can sign on for. Once you've signed on, you are committed to stay with the ship for that period. Except in extraordinary circumstances, such as serious illness, leaving the ship before your tour is up ("jumping ship") can bring financial and other penalties. And when you join a ship in the United States, you are only to leave it in the United States.

At sea, sailors work in shifts around the clock. Typically, they work ("stand watch") for four hours, then are off for eight hours, seven days a week. In-port watches are eight hours on, sixteen off. They work in all weather conditions. There are hazards that can mean injury or death—fire, collision, sinking, falling overboard, or working with heavy machinery, heavy loads, and dangerous cargo.

Newer vessels are air-conditioned, soundproofed from noisy machinery, and equipped with comfortable living quarters. Even so, the long periods away from home and the confinement aboard ship send some sailors ashore for good.

The world you get to see in your travels on a merchant ship may not be quite what you imagine. Because today's seagoing cargo carriers operate on tight schedules, you might not have much time ashore at the port calls your ship makes around the world.

A ship's typical routine is to arrive in a port and stand off its docks until space is available for the ship to dock and unload or take on cargo, which is done in the fastest possible time to make up for the waiting time at anchor. Loading operations often continue around the clock. "You might wait on the hook [at anchor] for hours or weeks," says one deckhand.

Once at the dock, huge modern container ships can be loaded and unloaded fairly quickly, perhaps within a day. It can take three or four days to load or unload ships carrying bulk cargo, such as coal and grain.

When crew members go ashore, they usually are required to stay within twenty-five miles of the port city. In many cases, the ship's crew may have only a few hours to go ashore, and that means they can't roam far beyond the dock area, usually not the most attractive part of a city. Nevertheless, following the sea will probably always have a certain adventurous appeal.

Marcel Scuderi joined the merchant marine when he was nineteen, fresh out of high school and Seafarers' Union training. In the four years he served aboard merchant ships, he visited thirty-three countries around the world. "These were my college years," he says.

"The experience couldn't be beat. You get to travel and make pretty decent money," says Scuderi. He preferred sailing on older freighters and tankers. "They do a lot of port hopping in a region of the world, and they stay in port longer than the newer, larger ships. The first ship I was on made eleven ports in two months' time."

In his four years on various ships, Scuderi visited Russia, Germany, Belgium, India, Japan, Singapore, Hong Kong, the West Coast of the United States, and ports in Africa and the Middle East. Eventually he decided to stay ashore, went to art school, and became a graphic designer.

Getting into the Merchant Marine

Deck and engineering officers in the merchant marine must be licensed. To qualify for that license, applicants must have graduated from the U.S. Merchant Marine Academy at Kings Point, New York, or from one of the six state merchant marine academies. Their four-year programs lead to bachelor of science degrees. All applicants also must pass a license exam. Licensed merchant marine officers may also qualify for commissions as U.S. Coast Guard Reserve officers.

Three years of appropriate sea experience can be substituted for this schooling. This requirement is not met easily or quickly by most. Since sailors may actually work only six months a year, or less, racking up the requisite sea experience can take five to eight years. And the license exam is difficult to pass without substantial formal schooling or independent study.

Education and experience are important at all stages in the merchant marine. To advance from third officer to a higher rank also requires experience and passing scores on additional exams. Because of the stiff competition for ship's officer positions, candidates often take a job below the one they are qualified for just to get in line for the better position.

Is just signing on and sailing off on a merchant ship still possible? In a way, it is. In order to become what's called an unlicensed seaman—the bottom rung on the merchant marine ladder—you need a merchant mariner's document. All that is required to get it is U.S. citizenship and a U.S. Public Health Service medical certificate stating you have good color perception and are in good general physical condition. Although no experience or formal schooling is required, training at a school operated by the Seafarers' International Union of North America, AFL-CIO, can ease your way.

Applicants who are accepted are classified as ordinary seamen and may be assigned to the deck or engineering departments of U.S. merchant ships. With experience at sea, and more union-sponsored training, an ordinary seaman can become an able seaman by passing an exam.

No training, experience, or documentation is required to become a deckhand on vessels operating in U.S. harbors, rivers, and similar waterways. This is where many would-be deep-sea sailors begin to accumulate the on-the-job experience they need to eventually qualify for a merchant marine license.

Entry, training, and educational requirements for most water transportation occupations are established and regulated by the U.S. Coast Guard.

Job Outlook

After several years of decline, employment in the deep-sea shipping industry has stabilized. Jobs will grow more slowly than average, and this growth will vary by sector of the field. Jobs aboard oceangoing ships bring high pay, but competition for these jobs remains keen. Merchant mariners may have to wait months between work opportunities.

New international regulations have raised shipping standards in the area of safety, training, and working conditions. Consequently, U.S. flagships should get more business, and hire more merchant mariners, as competition decreases from ships that sail under foreign flags of convenience and don't meet the new maritime standards. At the same time, new technology allows ships to sail with fewer crew members at the controls.

Many experienced merchant mariners go long periods without work. Unions generally are accepting fewer new members than in the past.

Annual pay for a ship captain of a large vessel, such as a container ship, oil tanker, or passenger ship, may exceed $100,000 after many years of experience. On the basis of a forty-hour week, the median annual salary for a captain is $70,242; for engineers, $47,528; for deck sailors and oilers, $28,122.

For More Information

Maritime Administration
U.S. Department of Transportation
400 Seventh Street SW, Room 7302
Washington, DC 20590
www.marad.dot.gov

Seafarer's International Union of North America
5201 Auth Way
Camp Springs, MD 20746
www.seafarers.org

Paul Hall Center for Maritime Training and Education
Lundeberg School of Seamanship
P.O. Box 75
Piney Point, MD 20674
www.seafarers.org/phc

International Organization of Masters, Mates, and Pilots
700 Maritime Boulevard
Linthicum Heights, MD 21090
www.bridgedeck.org

U.S. Merchant Marine Academy
Admissions Office
300 Steamboat Road
Kings Point, NY 11024
www.usmma.edu

U.S. Coast Guard Maritime Center
Licensing and Evaluation Branch
4200 Wilson Boulevard, Suite 630
Arlington, VA 22203
www.uscg.mil

Truck, Tour Bus, and Train Drivers

···

Truckers and the Open Road

The dream trip of many who long to travel is to motor across the land, observing the sweeping panorama of the landscape from highways and byways, free to stop wherever and whenever they fancy. "Now that's traveling!" they would say.

In a manner of speaking, you can take that trip—and get paid for it—as an over-the-road truck driver. From a perch six feet or so above the road, the driver of an eighteen-wheel tractor-trailer rig sees a panorama beyond the view of travelers in cars. All of America is open to the exploration of long-haul truckers. During some part of its journey from producer to consumer, nearly everything is transported for some distance by trucks. Goods may also be shipped between terminals or warehouses in distant cities and countries by ship, plane, or train, but trucks usually do the hauling from factories to cargo terminals and from transfer points to stores and even homes.

Long-distance truck drivers are common on the nation's interstates and major connecting highways. Their rigs—some with two or three tandem trailers—jockey for position in an effort to maintain a steady speed. Technology has made truck cabs more comfortable and the work of driving less physically demanding. Drivers communicate with their shipping agents via satellite communication links and use global positioning systems (GPS) to select the best routes to their destinations as well as check on weather and road conditions.

The Daily Routine

Long-distance truck drivers are often away from home in their travels. On some long runs, where pickups and deliveries are far apart, shipping companies use two drivers (sometimes a husband-and-wife team). One drives while the other sleeps in a berth compartment behind the cab of the truck. These "sleeper" runs may last for days—even weeks—with the truck usually stopping only for fuel, food, loading, and unloading. It's not unheard of for a self-employed driver to spend a year on the road between visits to home.

On the other hand, some truckers have regular runs, transporting freight to the same cities on a regular basis. These trips can seem like just another day at the office but with constantly changing scenery outside your "office" windows!

Long-distance truck drivers spend most of their working time behind the wheel, but the job doesn't end when they step out of the cab at the end of a trip. When drivers reach the destination, or the end of an operating shift, they complete reports about the trip and the condition of the truck. If there were any accidents, they have to file detailed reports about them.

Drivers may also unload the cargo at the destination. For example, drivers of rigs that haul household furnishings around the country usually help with the loading and unloading at each end of the journey. They may hire several local day workers to help them. Some take helpers along on long runs.

Work hours and other operating rules for interstate truckers are regulated by the U.S. Department of Transportation. For example, those rules stipulate that a long-distance driver cannot be on duty for more than sixty hours in any seven-day period and cannot drive more than ten hours straight, which must be followed by at least eight consecutive hours off duty. Many drivers, particularly on long runs, work close to the maximum number of hours permitted.

Getting into the Business

Most truck drivers are employed by trucking companies or by manufacturing and distribution companies that have fleets of trucks to move the goods they make or sell. Fewer than one out of ten truck drivers is self-employed. Of these owner operators, some operate independently, serving a variety of clients, while others lease their services and their trucks to trucking companies for assignment.

State and federal regulations set qualifications and standards for truck drivers. All state regulations must meet federal standards; some state rules are more stringent than the federal regulations. At the very least, all truck drivers must have a driver's license issued by the state where they live, and most employers also prefer drivers who have good driving records. In most cases, tractor-trailer drivers are required to obtain a special commercial driver's license (CDL) from the state where they live. All truckers who haul hazardous materials must have a CDL.

To obtain the CDL, you must pass a knowledge test and demonstrate that you can operate a commercial truck safely. All driving violations incurred by persons who hold commercial licenses are recorded permanently in a national data bank, so a driver whose commercial license is suspended or revoked in one state will find it difficult, if not impossible, to obtain a new one from another state.

Until they get the CDL, driver trainees must be accompanied by a driver with a CDL whenever they are behind the wheel of a truck. The Transportation Department stipulates the minimum qualifications for truck drivers engaged in interstate commerce: a driver must be at least twenty-one years old and pass a physical exam (employers usually pay for this) that shows the driver has good hearing, 20/40 vision with or without glasses, normal use of arms and legs, and normal blood pressure. In addition, drivers must pass a written exam on the motor carrier safety regulations of the Transportation Department.

Many trucking companies have higher standards. They may require drivers to be high school graduates and at least twenty-five years old with three to five years of experience as a truck driver. Many require annual physical exams for their drivers and may require drivers to submit to periodic drug screening as a condition of employment.

There are schools that train drivers, and they're not like those driver's ed courses for new motorists. Dealing with the multiple gears, the brakes, and the instrumentation of an eighteen-wheeler rig takes training and practice. Some truckers learn these skills in the armed forces.

In addition to their truck driving skills and experience, owner operators must have good business sense. Successful independent operators take courses in accounting, business, and similar subjects to be able to tackle all the paperwork involved in the business, and they often have a good knowledge of truck mechanics, which enables them to perform their own routine maintenance and do minor repairs on their rigs.

Employment Outlook

The U.S. Department of Labor predicts that jobs for truck drivers will increase as fast as the average for all occupations, as a strong economy requires ever-increasing transfers of goods. This occupation has among the greatest number of job openings every year. The exact number of openings at any time will vary because the amount of freight carried by trucks fluctuates with the economy. During economic slowdowns, some truck drivers may be laid off, and others may see their earnings drop with reduced work time or shipments. Owner operators tend to be hit especially hard by slowdowns.

Truckers' earnings vary widely depending on weekly work hours, number of nights that must be spent on the road, and the type and size of the equipment they operate. As with most professions, competition is stronger for the jobs with the best pay and working conditions.

As a rule, long-distance drivers are paid by the mile, and the rate can vary widely from employer to employer. Earnings increase with total mileage, seniority with the company, and the size and type of truck drivers handle (most long-distance drivers operate tractor-trailers). Many companies also offer their drivers bonuses for good safety and on-time-delivery records. Earnings for long-haul drivers typically range from $9.50 to $19.00 an hour, with the highest-paid 10 percent of drivers making $22.50 or more per hour. A driver near the top of the wage scale who averages six days of work a week and takes three weeks off during the year might earn $66,000 annually. A typical self-employed long hauler might have net earnings of $20,000 to $25,000 a year after deducting living expenses and other costs associated with operating the truck.

Many truck drivers are members of the International Brotherhood of Teamsters, Chauffeurs, Warehousemen and Helpers of America—the Teamsters, for short.

For More Information

The Teamsters Union
25 Louisiana Avenue NW
Washington, DC 20001
www.teamsters.org
> (Or check your telephone directory for the local union office.)

American Trucking Associations
2200 Mill Road
Alexandria, VA 22314
www.truckline.com

Professional Truck Driver Institute
2200 Mill Road
Alexandria, VA 22314
www.ptdi.org

....

Tour Bus Drivers

If you decide that long-distance truck driving isn't the kind of travel job you want, maybe driving a tour bus (motorcoach, in the vernacular of the business) will interest you. If it is the most glorious vistas and experiences you want to take in, this job can deliver.

The bus driver's job differs from the truck driver's work. For one thing, the itineraries of tour bus drivers link popular sightseeing, recreation, and entertainment destinations rather than city warehouse districts. The pace is usually more leisurely than that of truck drivers, although tour bus drivers may work nights, weekends, and holidays, just as truck drivers do.

Since they deal with human passengers, bus drivers must be able to get along well with people. The job requires them to be courteous. They need an even temperament and emotional stability to handle driving in heavy, fast-moving, and stop-and-go traffic—and to deal with passengers' needs and comfort. Drivers often must act as customer service representatives, tour guides, program directors, and safety advisors.

However, because they sometimes carry the same passengers throughout a tour, which may last for a week or longer, tour bus drivers often share pleasant memories with their passengers. This chance to get to know the passengers can make the job more pleasant than driving a bus on a regular inter-city schedule.

Getting into the Business

Like truck drivers, bus drivers must comply with state and U.S. Department of Transportation (DOT) rules and requirements and pass an exam on motor carrier safety regulations of the DOT. They must obtain a Commercial Driver's License (CDL), just as truck drivers do, and bus drivers must meet health, age, and training standards comparable to those of truck drivers. Bus drivers should be able to handle some cargo, too—handling passengers' suitcases, which are stowed in luggage compartments underneath the passenger deck of the bus, is part of the job.

Tour bus drivers typically work for charter companies, which in turn are hired by tour companies to provide buses with drivers for specific itineraries. Some tour bus drivers may work directly for tour operators who run bus tours in major cities, tourist regions, or on routes that cross the country. Still other drivers have their own equipment and hire themselves and their motorcoaches to travel and tour agencies.

The work may be seasonal, since the major tourist travel time is May through September, although travel is becoming more year-round now, especially in long-weekend lengths. Of course, in major Sunbelt areas, pleasure travel is a year-round business, and there may also be seasonal peaks in winter months.

Employment Outlook

Employment for tour bus drivers is very competitive. The amount of available work can vary, as the travel business is highly sensitive to the whims of the economy, weather, and other factors. Jobs are projected to grow at an average pace over the next decade.

Median earnings of tour bus drivers are comparable to those of inter-city bus drivers and can depend on the number of miles they drive. Wages range from $9.47 to $16.78 an hour, with a median of $12.36. The top 10 percent of drivers make $20 or more an hour. Those who work about six months a year can earn about $20,000, while senior drivers who work year-round might earn more than $40,000.

Drivers employed by tour operators and charter companies may enjoy health and life insurance and other fringe benefits. For those who are travel buffs, an additional benefit is being able to visit the country's prime tourist destinations—usually in ideal weather and with interesting people.

For More Information

The Teamsters Union
25 Louisiana Avenue NW
Washington, DC 20001
www.teamsters.org
   (Or check your telephone directory for the local union office.)

National Tour Association
546 East Main Street
Lexington, KY 40508
www.ntaonline.com

American Bus Association
1100 New York Avenue NW, Suite 1050
Washington, DC 20005
www.buses.org

United Motorcoach Association
113 South West Street
Alexandria, VA 22314
www.uma.org

Also ask travel agents for the names of tour operators who offer bus tours in the United States and Canada, such as Maupintour of Lawrence, Kansas, and Tauck Tours of Westport, Connecticut.

....

Engineers, Conductors, and the Romance of Railroading

Nearly every American schoolchild learns about the driving of the golden stake that completed the transcontinental railroad at

Promontory Point, Utah. And rightfully so, as the railroad soon became the lifeline of this young country. In a country so vast, trains meant easier communication, travel, and trade. The sight of a steam locomotive chugging across the prairie is an iconic American image. And while train travel has declined in America over the years, the romance of rail travel lingers. For many people, there is something special about a scenic train trip—the soothing click clack of steel wheels on steel rails, wilderness panoramas viewed from sky dome cars, cozy sleeping compartments, the pleasures of dining and bar cars.

The most popular passenger railroad routes in North America are those of Amtrak and Via Rail Canada that offer unparalleled scenic vistas—primarily those in the great northwestern expanse of rocky mountains, high meadows, and icy peaks on both sides of the United States–Canada border.

The Life of a Railroader

Engineers are the top brass on train trips. Because they're in the driver's seat, they are thoroughly knowledgeable about the rail system, signals, and terminals along the route, and they must be constantly aware of the condition and makeup of the train. Trains react differently to acceleration, braking, and curves, depending on the number of cars, the ratio of empty to loaded cars, and the amount of slack in the train. Engineers operate locomotives in rail yards, at train stations, and on the railroad between terminals. Most run diesel locomotives; a few run electric locomotives.

The engineer's chief aide is the conductor. On freight trains, conductors keep records of each car's contents and destination and make sure cars are added and removed at the right points along the route. On passenger trains, conductors also collect tickets and fares and assist passengers. At stops, they signal engineers, telling them when to pull out of the station. On key Amtrak runs, there may be a conductor and several assistant conductors.

Before a train leaves its originating terminal, the railroad company's dispatcher gives the conductor and engineer instructions on the train's route, timetable, and cargo. The engineer and conductor discuss plans for the trip. Once underway, the conductor may receive additional information by radio about track conditions ahead or the need to pull off the main track at the next available stop so another train can pass. The conductor then uses a two-way radio to contact the engineer and relay this and other information and instructions received from dispatchers and to remind the engineer of stops, reported track conditions, and the presence of other trains.

Since most trains operate twenty-four hours a day, many railroad employees work nights, weekends, and holidays. Seniority usually dictates who gets the more desirable shifts. As a general rule, passenger-train workers have the most regular and reliable shifts and most comfortable working conditions.

Getting into the Business

Most railroad workers begin as trainees for either engineer or brake-operator jobs. Railroads prefer that applicants for these jobs have a high school education and mechanical aptitude and be in good physical condition—with good hearing, eyesight and color vision, eye-hand coordination, and manual dexterity. Applicants must pass a physical exam and tests that screen for drug use.

Most beginning engineers undergo six-month training programs that include classroom and on-the-job instruction. From that point, they work their way up to top engineer positions.

Conductor jobs usually are filled from the ranks of experienced brake operators who have passed tests covering signals, timetables, operating rules, and related subjects. Some companies require that candidates pass these tests within the first few years of employment in order to advance.

About 80 percent of railroad workers are members of unions and have relatively high earnings.

If you want a job that keeps you rolling over the rails, you can become a locomotive engineer or conductor on a freight train or

Amtrak or Via Rail Canada passenger train. Or, go after one of the passenger-service jobs on these trains, such as bartender, cook, or waiter in the dining and bar cars, or host on long-distance sleeper trains.

Employment Outlook

Especially in the United States, employment opportunities for the majority of railroad workers will decline through the rest of this decade and beyond. Only engineer jobs will grow, but slowly. Overall employment in the industry continues to decline for several reasons. For one thing, demand is decreasing for railroad services because of price competition from airlines, bus, and truck lines. In addition, innovations such as larger, faster, more fuel-efficient trains, computerized rail-yard systems, containerized shipping, and intermodal systems are making it possible for railroads to move freight more efficiently.

Computers are used to keep track of freight cars, match empty cars with the closest loads, dispatch trains, and feed information and instructions to engineers. This increased reliance on computers means the railroads need fewer employees than in the past to move freight.

While the future of commuter passenger trains between major cities in the Northeast United States appears good, the outlook is not as good for Amtrak's long-distance trains. In the years ahead, probably the only passenger trains outside the Northeast corridor will be the excursion trains—rail cruises—that are operated by various tour companies along the United States–Canada border. Via Rail Canada offers passenger rail service coast to coast in that country.

If you get a top job with a railroad company, salaries can be good. Annual earnings of locomotive engineers in passenger service average $81,000. For engineers in freight service, the average is $61,400. Conductors in passenger service average $68,300 a year; those in freight service average $53,500.

For More Information

Brotherhood of Locomotive Engineers
1370 Ontario Street, Mezzanine
Cleveland, OH 44113
www.ble.org

Brotherhood of Locomotive Engineers
National Legislative Board Canada
Suite 1401, 150 Metcalf Street
Ottawa, ON K2P 1P1
Canada
www.ble.org/canada

United Transportation Union
International Headquarters
14600 Detroit Avenue
Cleveland, OH 44107
www.utu.org

United Transportation Union
Canadian Headquarters
National Office
Seventh Floor, 71 Bank Street
Ottawa, ON K1P 5N2
Canada
www.utu-canada.com

Association of American Railroads
50 F Street NW
Washington, DC 20001
www.aar.org

Amtrak, National Passenger Railroad Corporation
Human Resources Department
60 Massachusetts Avenue NE
Washington, DC 20002
www.amtrak.com

Via Rail Canada
3 Place Ville-Marie, Suite 500
Montreal, QC H3B 2C9
Canada
www.viarail.ca

CHAPTER FIVE

Business Travelers

Top Executives

No matter what your field, when you reach the top echelons in the worlds of business and government, odds are great that your job will require you to travel frequently—to visit your lieutenants in the field, inspect far-flung offices and plants, attend conferences, and meet with major customers and constituents in locations around the world.

Chief executives of major corporations may even fly in their own corporate jets. At this level of the American workforce, when you work hard, you play hard as well. A business trip that takes you across the country might be extended for a day or two so you can play a little golf and unwind at a resort. Also, when heads of industry travel to conferences and meetings, their spouses may accompany them.

What are the jobs that offer these perks? They are the positions of corporate chairperson, chief executive officer, and various second-tier executives, such as chief operating and financial officers plus vice presidents and other executives and managers of major plants, stores, and regional and branch offices. Many top-tier lawyers, physicians, college presidents, real-estate developers, and financial dealers also operate in this style.

As you'll see later in this chapter, so do many politicians and government officials. But unlike private-sector executives, the working routines of government chiefs are subject to wide public scrutiny through the media. And they risk scandal and fall from power if they indulge in an executive work style that is too fancy for the taxpayers to tolerate.

The Daily Routine

In jobs at the top of the management hierarchy, you formulate policy and direct the operations of companies and government agencies. An organization's chief executive collaborates with its board of directors and other top executives to move the entity on its course. In a large corporation, a busy CEO meets frequently with top executives of other corporations, government agencies, bankers, lawyers, and major customers. The work of running the operation is delegated to scores, even hundreds, of managers. How many top execs there are depends on the size and scope of the enterprise, of course.

Some multimillion-dollar organizations are run by a tightly knit group of several dozen managers in a single location. Other corporations are mammoth—with hundreds of top executives occupying a skyscraper and hundreds more in scores of plants and branch offices around the country or around the world.

Top executives may be provided with spacious offices and numerous perquisites, such as private dining rooms, cars, club memberships, and liberal expense accounts. These are meant to facilitate executives' meetings and negotiations with other corporate chiefs, customers, government regulators, and ministers of foreign countries where the company has assets.

Of course, it's not all three-hour lunches and limo rides at the top. Long workdays, including evenings and weekends, are the rule for most heads of industry. You might say they are always on call. Business discussions may occupy most of an executive's time at social engagements, on the golf course, or while fishing on an important client's yacht. It's hard to tell where business life ends and private life begins for many industry chiefs.

In large corporations, job transfers between headquarters and far-flung corporate plants, offices, and subsidiaries are common.

To climb to a top post in a major corporation, you might move your household to a new city five or six times over twenty years. Spouses and children have to adjust to this mobile life.

Managers work under often intense pressure to attain goals in production and sales, for instance. You can find yourself in situations in which you have limited influence—for example, meeting new requirements of government regulations, dealing with unexpected pressures from competitors or public-interest groups, or facing natural or financial catastrophes.

Travel is practically a given in the corporate world. Airlines created frequent-flyer clubs and programs—with discount rewards, special creature comforts, and other enticements—to capture their share of the travel time and dollars of this peripatetic group of workers who keep airplane seats filled throughout each workweek. In a global economy, American and Canadian managers conduct business around the world. Corporate executives and government bureaucrats travel between regional and local offices in the United States and overseas. To keep up with developments in their fields and network with their peers, executives regularly attend meetings and conferences in locations far from the home office.

Because work keeps them on the road so frequently, many of those conferences are held at properties where the management personnel can relax together after their work sessions—at receptions and dinners, golf and tennis matches, and the like. Many top executives are reimbursed for the traveling expenses of their accompanying spouses, since the wives and husbands of corporate managers often participate with them in corporate socializing.

Getting into the Management Stratosphere

The educational background of top executives varies as widely as the nature of their diverse responsibilities. Most of them have college degrees. Graduate and professional degrees are common in this group, especially the master of business administration (M.B.A.) and master of public administration (M.P.A.).

On the other hand, the degree may not be related to the executive's present field of work. And some top execs got to their lofty positions by dint of their own personal genius or hard work and have little formal schooling of any kind.

But if you want to plot a course for becoming a world-traveling corporate executive, your odds will be greatest if you have an appropriate college degree—such as business administration, public services or education administration, economics, finance, statistics, psychology, urban studies, or the like. A degree will help you get into position to climb the corporate management ladder.

However, making the climb usually calls for much more than simply an appropriate degree. Most top executive positions are filled by promoting experienced lower-level managers who display the leadership, self-confidence, motivation, decisiveness, personality, and corporate loyalty required in the executive suites.

In small firms, where the number of positions is limited, advancement to the upper strata of management can be slow. In giant firms, promotions may come more quickly, as there are many more intermediate levels where you can prepare for a top management position. Another feature of larger firms is that there are often company training programs that broaden your knowledge of company policy and operations in a timely fashion and thereby accelerate your passage through the hierarchy.

There is more than one path to the top. Instead of joining a company as an entry-level employee and working your way up the ladder there, you might climb faster by hopping from company to company or by starting your own firm after learning what you need to know at the big corporation.

As a rule, to become a top-tier manager, you should have highly developed personal skills, an analytical mind able to quickly assess large amounts of information, and the ability to consider and evaluate the interrelationship of numerous factors and select a successful course of action. You should also have sound intuitive judgment and be able to communicate clearly and persuasively, both orally and in writing.

Your Future in Top Management

The stock market bust at the start of this century put a lot of business chiefs out of work. Nevertheless, employment of top managers and executives should increase at an average pace through the end of this decade as businesses grow in number, size, and complexity. However, as competition intensifies internationally, and many firms improve operating efficiency by expanding individual managers' responsibilities, that could moderate employment growth in the top corporate ranks.

Executive employment growth will vary by industry, too. For example, most services industries will continue to expand. And employment growth is expected in firms that supply management, consulting, public relations, personnel, and other business services because more firms will find it cost efficient to contract out for these services. Executive employment should also grow in accounting, bookkeeping, and auditing services firms and in industries concerned with health and welfare, such as outpatient clinics and agencies offering individual and family social services.

There may be little or no growth—possibly even a decline in employment—in some manufacturing industries where business is being lost to foreign plants.

Top business executives are among the highest-paid workers there are. Long hours and considerable travel are part of their jobs. But their working quarters are very commodious, and they have many assistants. Salary levels of top executives vary substantially depending on many variables—the exec's managerial responsibility, length of service, particular specialty and experience, and the type, size, and location of the firm.

Most salaried executives in the private sector receive additional compensation in the form of bonuses, stock awards or options, and a variety of cash-equivalent fringe benefits, such as insurance premiums, physical examinations, country club memberships, use of company cars, and the usual paid vacation time, sick leave, and pensions. Many top executives in government and not-for-profit organizations receive similar benefits.

Salaries also vary substantially by industry and geographic location. For example, salaries in manufacturing and finance are generally higher than those for corresponding executive positions in state and local government. Salaries in large metropolitan areas are normally higher than those in small cities and towns. Some surveys of executive salaries reveal that a top manager in a very large corporation can earn ten times as much as a counterpart in a small firm.

CEOs—chief executive officers—are the most highly paid top-level managers. The estimated median annual salary of top business executives is about $114,000, and many earn much more. Surveys of major corporations show that hundreds of CEOs receive base salaries of a million dollars or more, plus additional compensation, such as fringe benefits and company stock, equivalent on the average to nearly half of their base salaries.

For CEOs of not-for-profit organizations, the estimated median salary is $75,000, but a few top associations pay their chief executives $450,000 or more. And these executives receive many of the perks of their counterparts in the for-profit sector.

With that kind of money, you can travel anywhere in the world without undue strain on the pocketbook.

For More Information

American Management Association
1601 Broadway
New York, NY 10019
www.amanet.org

National Management Association
2210 Arbor Boulevard
Dayton, OH 45439
www.nma1.org

International Personnel Management Association
1617 Duke Street
Alexandria, VA 22314
www.ipma-hr.org

....

Politicians

Another way to travel in your work is to get elected or appointed to public office at the state or national level. The president of the United States has probably the largest executive jet in the world, and when the president travels, they really do roll out a red carpet.

Governors, lieutenant governors, members of the U.S. Congress, and chiefs of top-level state and federal bureaus and departments routinely travel on business. Their travel patterns are similar to those of their corporate cousins in the private sector.

Government executives and elected officials make study trips, often with spouses and staff associates, to exotic and workaday destinations around the world—to attend conferences, solicit business investment or tourism from other states and countries, look at how U.S. aid is being spent in foreign lands, or meet with their counterparts in other governments. As mentioned earlier, if too lavish, such trips sometimes create negative publicity for politicians. Occasionally, media critics describe some of these trips as extravagant and unnecessary junkets, on which the public servants are wining and dining at extraordinary expense to the taxpayers.

Legislators receive allowances for travel from Washington, or their state capitals, to their home districts during the year. Many U.S. senators and representatives also travel around the country for speaking engagements, where they might receive an honorarium. their travel expenses are often covered by the host groups or political action committees (PACs), which are major sources of travel and entertainment money for politicians.

Salaries for governors range from $65,000 in Nebraska to $179,000 in New York. The highest-paid 10 percent of state legislators earn about $62,900 a year. Mayors of cities earn $92,338 on average. For county managers, the average is $107,500. U.S. senators and members of Congress are paid $145,100 per year. The U.S. vice president receives $181,000, and the president makes $400,000.

Getting yourself into such a position can be a long and arduous process of working with local political organizations for a chance to be nominated to run for office or be appointed to one. Politicians raise a lot of money to pay for election campaigns, which are risky. There are as many losers as winners, and both have to pump dollars into their campaigns.

Even the path to a top appointive government job, such as head of a department or agency, can require years of volunteer work and networking or being well connected to a politician who is in a position to make the appointments you covet.

Preparing for a shot at being a top government executive is similar to preparing for top jobs in the corporate world. But the road to the top in government is less structured. It can be traversed more quickly (if your candidate wins, you can gain an appointed job overnight), but it is usually more chancy than advancement in the world of commerce.

· ·

Meeting Planners

Obviously, meeting planners plan meetings. That might sound simple to you—until you recognize that these meetings aren't just for several people conversing across a desk or conference table. The meetings in question are usually major affairs involving hundreds to thousands of people at sites around the world. They are conventions, expositions, and trade shows.

Indeed, planning and running such meetings is a gigantic industry. Just think about all the businesses involved in putting on national or international conventions—hotels and convention centers, of course, and caterers, restaurants, printers of posters and program books, phone companies that rig up communication systems, bus and cab lines to haul delegates around, security services to keep them safe, musicians and other entertainers, audiovisual firms that put together slide shows, airlines that serve the convention city, and more. A major convention may draw ten thousand or more people. And it can pump hundreds of thousands of dollars into the economy of a city. It's been estimated that more than $35 billion is spent each year in the United States on meetings.

The people who organize these big operations are professional meeting planners. It's a relatively new occupation, but one that is solidly established in the business world today. Meeting planners perform a variety of functions in mounting conferences, from preparing a budget for the operation and selecting the site and facilities for the meeting to creating the meeting program, marketing the event to likely attendees, and actually running the meeting at the site.

They travel to dozens of cities to check out convention facilities and negotiate group rates for hotel accommodations, meals, and air and ground transportation for thousands of delegates who will attend the meetings. Planners set up a system for registering delegates in advance and booking their room reservations. They plan food and beverage functions, book entertainment for convention events, coordinate the production of printed and audiovisual materials, set up meeting and conference rooms, engage speakers, and organize trade shows with hundreds of exhibitors.

On the Job

Most U.S. associations and large corporations have a meeting planner or staff of planners. Many planners back into the profession; they become experts at planning meetings because they're required to arrange meetings for their companies, even though they weren't trained to do so. Their primary duties may have been in public relations or marketing or in other administrative areas.

But as meetings became a more important and costly function for businesses, the people assigned to manage them have become increasingly professional at this job. Meeting planners tend to be well-educated people who are making a career of this corporate function. Typically they have college degrees, working knowledge of the travel industry, and effective written and verbal communication skills. Meeting planners must interact well with all types of people and make important decisions even under pressure.

By far the greatest number of meeting planners are employed by corporations and by trade and professional associations. But there are some independent planners who work as consultants to companies that need meetings planned but do not have people within their organizations who can handle that duty.

Getting into the Business

An effective meeting planner must know how to function as a businessperson first and then specifically as a meeting planner. The background usually required of a meeting planner includes a four-year college degree, preferably in business administration, marketing, management, or communication. Some planners come from college programs in hotel management.

Beyond college, professional development programs and advanced training are available to planners through associations and other organizations in the field.

Often, getting your first job as a meeting planner is tough without experience. But how do you get experience if you can't get the job? Many planners do it by working in the convention sales office at a hotel, where hosting business meetings is a major source of revenue. Others work as interns or assistants to planners. Some gain experience by volunteering to plan activities such as office parties, community organization events, and church outings. Even if you don't get paid for your work, the experience is valid.

Landing a job as a professional meeting planner is very competitive. To be successful at it, you need a strategy for scouting out potential employers, then finding effective ways to make your pitch to them. For leads, consult directories of associations, since nearly every trade association has meetings and needs meeting planners.

Meeting Professionals International is the industry's leading educational and networking organization. It promotes the professional development of meeting planners through its own programs and meetings around the world. Planners with an adequate amount of working experience in the field who complete certain professional requirements can earn the designation of Certified Meeting Professional, a credential that greatly enhances their employability.

Your Future as a Meeting Planner

Professional meeting planners will find employment in the field growing faster than average. Americans, and people of many other countries throughout the world, are meeting more often at events and conferences that require professional planning, operation, and on-site coordination.

With the growing emphasis on adult and continuing education and the need for networking and exchanging information in all fields of work, meetings play a key role in giving attendees a competitive edge in their careers. This trend promotes continued demand for qualified meeting planners.

The positions meeting planners hold in companies and associations vary. Most are in the middle-management sphere, but a good number work in top-level management positions. Of course, salaries vary accordingly. Annual salaries for meeting planners range from $32,550 to $67,630. The median salary is $47,000; the highest-paid 10 percent of planners may earn $90,000 a year or more, depending on the size of the industry serve, the size of the corporation, and the geographic location.

For More Information

Meeting Professionals International
4455 LBJ Freeway, Suite 1200
Dallas, TX 75244
www.mpiweb.org

MPI Canadian Office
329 March Road
Suite 232, Box 11
Kanata, ON K2K 2E1
Canada

Corporate Sales Representatives

Once upon a time, the image of the traveling salesman was of a huckster toting a sample case full of kitchen utensils door to door in residential neighborhoods. Today's traveling salespeople may circle the world in pursuit of multimillion-dollar contracts for power plants, high-tech electronics, and custom-designed computer systems. Obviously, all salespeople aren't globe-trotters, but most who work for major companies find that travel is a way of life in their jobs. And as markets become more global, national boundaries fall.

Think of the thousands of products that are sold and bought each day—from bags of potato chips, romance novels, and sneakers to precision computer chips, giant construction equipment, and thousands of other products. The makers of the products employ sales representatives to market their products to manufacturers, distributors and wholesalers, retail stores, government agencies, and other institutions. They deal with buyers and purchasing agents.

Depending on where they work, these sales reps have different job titles. Most are referred to as manufacturers' or wholesale reps;

those who sell technical products may be called industrial sales reps or engineers.

Manufacturers', wholesale, and industrial sales reps may be employees of the firms whose goods and services they sell, or they may be self-employed agents who contract their services to various companies. Often contract reps specialize in selling particular lines of products and services. Some self-employed reps create their own companies and employ scores of salespeople who service client manufacturers.

The Daily Routine

Manufacturers' reps spend much of their time traveling to the offices and plants of prospective buyers. During sales calls, they show samples, pictures, and catalogs of items the company makes or stocks. They may discuss the customers' needs, then suggest how the company's merchandise can meet those needs.

Sales reps know about prices, availability, specifications, and performance of the products they sell and how they can save money and improve productivity for the buyers. Because of the vast number of manufacturers and wholesalers selling similar products and services, they might emphasize the prompt delivery and dependable follow-up services offered by their companies.

The sales reps usually are the people who must resolve any problems or complaints with the merchandise and services they sell. Often these manufacturers' reps sell products and services that must be custom designed for the buyers, who are usually large corporations. For example, selling computers to a company may mean designing a unique system of hardware, software, and peripheral equipment to handle a particular company's type of business. Or a machine product may have to be designed or modified to work in a certain way within a specific amount of space.

That's why manufacturers' sales reps often know much more about the field in which their products are used than do salespeople for consumer goods and less sophisticated merchandise.

Industrial sales engineers, for instance, usually are qualified engineers as well as sales agents. They typically sell products whose installation and optimal use require a great deal of technical expertise and support—industrial robots, mainframe computers, or manufacturing and assembly-line machinery.

In addition to providing information on their manufacturers' products, most reps help prospective buyers with technical problems and questions. For example, they might recommend improved materials and machinery for a customer's manufacturing process, draw up plans for how the proposed machinery would be used, and project cost savings that could result from the purchase of their equipment.

Such a sale isn't short and sweet. It may take weeks or months. It involves a process of negotiation. Salespeople present their proposals; the customer's managers react with questions or suggested modifications in the deal. The price is rarely fixed; it will depend on so many variables in the deal. The sales reps may work with engineers in their own companies, who adapt products to the customer's special needs. After the deal is done, the sales rep may make frequent follow-up visits to ensure that the equipment is functioning properly and may even get involved in training the customer's employees to operate and maintain the new equipment.

Of course, independent manufacturers' reps also manage their own businesses; they often have one or more employees who take care of accounting, marketing, and administrative matters.

Some manufacturers' and wholesale sales reps have large territories and do considerable traveling. Because a sales region may cover four or five states, they may be on the road for several days or weeks at a time.

Some rack up hundreds of thousands of airline miles every year. Others, who work near their home bases, may do most of their traveling by car. All of them certainly cover a lot of landscape. How much of it they get to appreciate may be another matter. For busy sales reps, days can be totally occupied making sales calls and many evenings spent writing reports and taking care of records. Traveling sales reps rarely work a standard forty-hour week.

Despite their often long and hectic hours, most sales reps have some freedom in determining their own schedules. They might arrange their appointments to allow some time off when they want it—and where they want it. And dealing with the variety of people you encounter in this level of sales work can be stimulating as well as demanding.

On the demanding side of the coin, sales reps operate in a fiercely competitive world. They must compete for business not only with reps from other companies, but often with other reps within their own organizations. Because their incomes depend largely, and often solely, on commissions, manufacturers' reps are under pressure to maintain and expand their client bases. Their companies may offer prizes and bonuses for reaching sales goals, but they also set sales quotas.

Getting into the Business

Two out of three reps work in wholesale trade—mostly for distributors of machinery and equipment, food products, motor vehicles and parts, hardware, plumbing, and electrical goods. Others work for manufacturers. Self-employed reps usually have gained experience and recognition with a manufacturer or wholesaler before going into business for themselves.

The background needed for these sales jobs varies by product line and market. A college degree usually is required, but many firms look mainly for previous sales experience. As a rule, the more sophisticated the product, the more educational preparation will be required for sales reps in that line. Firms selling industrial products may require that sales reps have a degree in science or engineering in addition to industry work experience.

Many companies have formal training programs for beginning sales reps that may last up to two years. Trainees might work in several jobs in the company's plants and offices to learn all phases of production, quality control, installation, and distribution. There might be classroom instruction followed by on-the-job training in branch offices under the supervision of field sales managers.

Manufacturers' reps should be goal oriented, have a persuasive but pleasant personality, and thrive on working independently. The ability to get along with people and problem-solving skills are a plus. Patience and perseverance are a must. And you should like traveling because you'll do a lot of it, visiting current and prospective clients.

Your Future as a Sales Rep

Employment of manufacturers' and wholesalers' representatives is expected to grow more slowly than average in the coming years. Ironically, the slowdown in job growth is caused by the increased efficiency of salespeople, largely through their use of new technologies. Also there is a trend to outsource the sales function to self-employed reps, whose pay often is based almost entirely on sales commissions.

In addition to having advancement possibilities within their own firms, the regular contact sales reps have with businesspeople in other firms may open up opportunities with other employers. Some sales reps eventually move into buying, purchasing, advertising, or marketing research. And there is always the option to go into business for oneself.

The income of most sales reps is based on a combination of salary and commission or bonus. Commissions usually are based on the amount of sales; bonuses may be tied to individual performance, the production of all sales workers in a group or district, or on the company's performance or goals.

Median annual earnings for manufacturers' representatives are about $40,340. The middle 50 percent earn between $28,850 and $57,280. The top 10 percent earn $82,830 or more.

Sales reps working for an employer usually are reimbursed for their travel and entertainment expenses and receive numerous benefits, including health and life insurance, a pension plan, vacation and sick leave, use of a company car, and frequent flyer mileage rewards. In addition, some companies offer incentives such as free trips or gifts for top sales performers.

Self-employed manufacturers' reps may have earnings significantly higher, or lower, than those of employee reps. It all depends on the client base and the cost-effectiveness of their operating and overhead expenses.

For More Information

Manufacturers' Agents National Association
P.O. Box 3467
23016 Mill Creek Drive
Laguna Hills, CA 92654
www.manaonline.org

Manufacturers' Representatives Educational Research
   Foundation
P.O. Box 247
Geneva, IL 60134
www.mrerf.org

CHAPTER SIX

Members of the Armed Forces and Law Enforcers

Military Service Men and Women

As the venerable recruiting slogan says, you can see the world as a member of the U.S. armed forces. Of course, you may see it from the inside of a Bradley fighting vehicle, an F-16 attack jet, or a naval ship at sea!

The mission of the armed forces is to deter aggression and defend the United States in times of conflict. That mission includes action overseas, such as the battles fought in the Middle East in the war against terrorism. In addition, the U.S. Coast Guard (under the U.S. Department of Transportation except in wartime, when it serves with the navy) enforces federal maritime laws, rescues distressed vessels and aircraft at sea, operates aids to navigation, and battles smugglers—nowadays, largely dope runners and terrorists—in the rivers and coastal waters of the United States.

To perform this mission, the military stations personnel at outposts around the world, from radar stations and intelligence listening posts in remote areas of the globe to major air, land, and sea bases that circle the world at strategic locations in countries allied with the United States.

At some foreign posts, members of the military may bring their families with them. And, on their off-duty time, they may tour the region like other sightseers and holiday travelers.

The Work

Just about any kind of job that exists in civilian society also exists in the military. Military personnel run hospitals, operate nuclear reactors, drive trucks, run ships. There are doctors, lawyers, ministers, secretaries, butchers, bakers, and aircraft and truck repairers in the service. Altogether, the armed forces are America's largest employer, with about 2.2 million persons on the active-duty payroll in normal times. The military services provide educational opportunities and work experience in literally thousands of occupations and at every career level.

Men and women in the service hold managerial and administrative jobs; professional, technical, and clerical jobs; construction jobs; electrical and electronics jobs; mechanical and repair jobs; and many others. In addition to jobs that have an equivalent in civilian life, the armed forces have jobs that are unique to the military, such as infantry specialists, artillery gun crews, and aircraft carrier catapult operators.

There are more than two thousand basic and advanced military occupational specialties for enlisted personnel and sixteen hundred for officers. They include the military jobs of infantry specialists, gun crews, and seamanship specialists who are the backbone of the services; functional support and administrative jobs that are similar to those in business and government, from personnel managers to payroll clerks; electronic equipment repairers; communications and intelligence specialists; service and supply workers; medical and dental technicians; civil engineers and architects; machinists, plumbers, welders, and other craft workers; and technical and specialty occupations, from public affairs officers and band directors to photographers and graphic designers.

Of all military personnel, about 21 percent work in electrical and mechanical equipment repair; 17 percent are infantry, gun crew, and seamanship specialists; 15 percent are in functional support and administrative jobs; 10 percent in electronic equipment repair; 10 percent in communications and intelligence; 9 percent in service and supply; 6 percent in medical and dental specialties; 4 percent are craftspeople; and 2 percent work in other technical and allied specialties.

Officers, who account for about 15 percent of all military personnel, are concentrated in administrative, medical, and dental specialties as well as in combat activities, where they serve as ships' officers, aircraft pilots and crew members, and infantry or artillery officers.

When you sign an enlistment contract, you sign a legal document that obligates you to serve for a specified period of time. Military life is more regimented than civilian life. Dress and grooming requirements are more stringent than in most civilian jobs, and rigid formalities govern many aspects of everyday life. For example, officers and enlisted personnel do not socialize together, and superior commissioned officers are saluted and addressed as "sir" or "ma'am." These and other rules encourage respect for superiors whose commands must be obeyed immediately and without question.

The needs of the military always come first. As a result, hours and working conditions can be quite different from the civilian workplace. As a rule, most military personnel work eight hours a day, five or five-and-a-half days a week. However, on a rotating basis, military personnel may have to work, or be on call, at night and on weekends. In the service, when you are called, no matter the time of day, you respond.

Travel is part of life for all members of the service. Depending on the branch of the service and your particular job in the military, you may spend considerable time traveling. For example, the officers and crews of naval ships roam the oceans and visit ports around the world. U.S. air and ground troops stationed overseas can spend their weekends and vacation time visiting the countries where they have been sent as part of their jobs.

U.S. military personnel are stationed throughout the United States and in many countries around the world. About 258,000 are stationed outside the United States. Most of these are posted in Europe, east Asia and the Pacific area, and on navy ships at sea.

While military duty certainly offers an opportunity to see the world, there are trade-offs for that travel. Your quarters on a military ship may be rather spartan. Your port calls may be limited. You may be confined to your ship, such as a nuclear submarine, for periods of months without any port call at all. And you are separated from your family when at sea or on active duty. But on a more positive note, you also gain the respect and gratitude of your country for volunteering to serve.

Despite its often resembling a civilian job, life in the military does always have an element of danger. Air and ground forces stationed overseas may be in isolated areas, in countries where there are few amenities, or in parts of the world subject to extremes of temperature and other conditions. Overseas troops may be in hazardous situations even when combat is not involved. Of course, there is always the possibility that you'll be engaged in combat. Sometimes military training activities can be almost as dangerous as war itself.

Signing Up

The U.S. military is a volunteer force. Enlisted members must sign a legal agreement that usually involves a commitment to eight years of service, with two to six of those years on active duty and the balance in the reserves. In return, the service provides a job, pay (plus cash bonuses for enlistment in certain occupations), medical and other benefits, training, and continuing education.

Applicants for enlistment must be seventeen to thirty-five years old (for the marines, the age limit is twenty-nine; for the Coast

Guard, twenty-eight), a U.S. citizen or immigrant alien holding permanent resident status with no felony record, pass written tests and medical exams, and have a high school diploma or equivalent for certain service options.

Officers enter the service through one of the military academies, where appointments come through members of Congress, through competitive examinations, and from Reserve Officer Training Corps (ROTC) programs at colleges and universities around the country. Upon graduation from the academies or ROTC training in college, officer candidates receive commissions in the services. College graduates who have not taken ROTC courses can apply for direct admission to the services through Officer Candidate School programs.

As military jobs become more technical and complex, educational requirements are rising. High school graduates and even those with some college background will be in demand for jobs in the enlisted ranks. Officers must have at least a four-year college degree, and certain occupational specialties require advanced degrees or degrees in particular fields.

Your Future in the Military

Opportunities are good in all branches of the armed forces for applicants who meet designated standards. About 365,000 enlisted personnel and officers are needed each year to replace those who retire or leave the armed forces for other reasons.

Military personnel enjoy more job security than their civilian counterparts. And in the years ahead, more attention probably will be paid to improving the quality of military life—with such things as shorter periods of sea duty and child-care facilities at land bases—as the armed forces look for ways to improve the retention of their personnel.

Starting salaries of military enlisted personnel with special skills range from $1,289 to $1,576 a month. For warrant officers, the pay range is $1,783 to $3,019 per month. For commissioned officers, the monthly range is $1,998 for a new officer to $11,049 for top generals and admirals with twenty years' service. The earnings of the bulk of the officer corps—captains and majors—range from $2,638 to $4,935 a month. Warrant officers' base pay ranges from $1,783 to $4,641 per month. Most enlisted personnel—specialists and sergeants—earn between $1,289 and $2,040 a month.

In addition to basic pay, benefits for military personnel include free room and board or housing and subsistence allowances, medical and dental care, a military clothing allowance, military supermarket and department store shopping privileges, thirty days of paid vacation per year, and opportunities for travel on military transportation.

Special pay generally is available for unusually demanding or hazardous duty, assignment to duties requiring skills in which there is a shortage, assignment to certain areas outside the continental United States, and for outstanding performance evaluations. Military personnel are eligible for retirement benefits after twenty years of service.

Other fringe benefits of the military life include athletic and other recreational facilities—such as gymnasiums, tennis courts, golf courses, bowling centers, libraries, and movie theaters—that are available at many military installations. Advice and assistance with personal or financial problems is also available through the services.

For More Information

The Department of Defense publishes a military career guide for students, and each of the service branches publishes handbooks, fact sheets, and pamphlets that describe entrance requirements, training and advancement opportunities, and other aspects of military careers. These publications are available at all recruiting stations, many state employment service offices, and in many high schools, colleges, and public libraries. Look in the local Yellow Pages for the location of recruiting offices for all branches of the armed forces.

Law Enforcement Agents

As the saying goes, in pursuit of justice, law enforcement officers may travel to the ends of the earth—tracking a wanted fugitive, clues to solve a crime, or intelligence on terrorist cells and plans. There are many branches in the field of law enforcement. Perhaps the one that first springs to mind when you are thinking about travel are the air marshals.

To assure air travel safety from terrorist attack, the Federal Aviation Administration's air marshals program expanded greatly after the terror attacks on America on September 11, 2001. Special teams of undercover air marshals fly aboard U.S. airline flights worldwide to watch for and meet terrorist challenges that may arise. Members of this elite corps must meet stringent physical standards and proficiencies. Only limited information about the program can be made public.

Federal Agents

Federal law enforcement agents are in a position to travel most as their jurisdiction extends well beyond local or state boundaries. In addition to the air marshals corps, the primary agencies are the Federal Bureau of Investigation (FBI), the U.S. Customs Service, the Central Intelligence Agency (CIA), the Bureau of Alcohol, Tobacco, and Firearms (ATF), and the U.S. Secret Service. Collectively, these are the legendary "G"-men and -women.

FBI agents investigate violations of federal law, typically bank robberies, theft of government property, organized crime, espionage, sabotage, kidnapping, and terrorism. Many of these cases are international in scope. Many agents work mainly on cases related to their areas of expertise. For example, agents with an accounting background may investigate white-collar crimes such as bank embezzlements and fraudulent bankruptcies or tracking the international movement of bank accounts and other assets by terrorist networks. FBI agents usually are called to testify in court about the cases they investigate.

The work of many CIA agents is clandestine. They work at posts around the world. Their accomplishments may never be known to anyone outside the U.S. intelligence services.

Customs agents enforce laws preventing the illegal smuggling of goods across U.S. borders. Alcohol, Tobacco, and Firearms agents investigate suspected illegal sales of guns and the underpayment of federal taxes by liquor or cigarette manufacturers.

A major responsibility of the U.S. Secret Service is to protect the president and vice president of the United States and their immediate families, as well as presidential candidates, ex-presidents, and foreign dignitaries visiting the United States. But Secret Service agents also are charged with investigating counterfeiting, forgery of government checks or bonds, and the fraudulent use of credit cards.

Obviously, Secret Service agents in the Presidential Protective Force log thousands of travel miles every year. They must accompany the president and vice president on their travels throughout the nation and around the world. And some squads from the presidential force travel in advance to locations the president plans to visit in order to check out potential hazards and figure out ways to avoid them.

Local and State Police

Police department detectives and special agents often go to great lengths—and travel great distances—to collect evidence for criminal cases, conduct interviews, examine records and crime scenes, observe the activities of suspects, and participate in raids and arrests.

And talk about hitting the road—state highway patrol officers do it every day. State troopers are responsible for patrolling state highways and federal interstates and enforcing the law within their states. Patrolling the highways that crisscross the country is not the only job of the state police, but it is probably the most visible. A state trooper's car is a welcome sight when you are stranded on the side of the road with car trouble and an upsetting sight when you're being pulled over for speeding after zipping past an unseen radar trap.

In addition to ticketing motorists who drive too fast and recklessly, state troopers give life-saving first aid, call for emergency help and vehicles, and direct traffic at accident scenes. They also write reports that may be used to determine the causes of accidents. For highway travelers in less serious need of help, the state police can radio for road service when drivers are having mechanical trouble.

Both state and local police officers provide traffic assistance and control during road repairs, fires, and other emergencies and during special occasions, such as parades and sports events. In some states, they check the weight of commercial vehicles at highway weighing stations, conduct driver licensing examinations, and distribute public reports on highway safety. When they're not on the road, state police officers may act as security guards for the governor and travel with the state's chief executive on all official trips in and out of the state.

In most states, state troopers also have a hand in enforcing state criminal laws. They may help city or county police track and catch lawbreakers and control civil disturbances. In communities and counties that do not have a local police force or large sheriff's department, the state police are the primary law enforcement agency, investigating crimes such as burglary, assault, and murder.

Getting into Law Enforcement

To be a police officer or federal agent, you should have a sense of public service and enjoy working with many different types of people. Various federal agencies—primarily the Treasury Department and the FBI—employ about 5 percent of special agents and law enforcement officers. State police agencies employ about 10 percent of all police, detectives, and special agents. The balance are employed by local police departments.

Civil service regulations govern the appointment of police officers in practically all states and large cities. Basically, candidates must perform well on competitive written examinations and meet requirements based on education and experience. They must also pass physical exams that test vision, strength, and agility.

Personal characteristics such as honesty, good judgment, and a sense of responsibility are especially important in police and detective work, so candidates are interviewed by a senior officer, and their character traits and backgrounds are usually investigated. For some police jobs, candidates are interviewed by psychiatrists or psychologists or are given personality tests. And most applicants are subjected to lie-detector exams and drug testing.

For many police jobs, you need only a high school education. But an increasing number of cities and states require some college training for these jobs, and some hire law enforcement students as police interns. More and more police departments are encouraging applicants to take post–high school training in law enforcement. Nowadays many entrants to police and detective jobs have completed some formal postsecondary education; a significant number are college graduates.

To be considered for appointment as an FBI special agent, an applicant must be a college graduate with a major in accounting, engineering, or computer science or have a law degree or be fluent in a foreign language. College graduates who don't have specialized degrees must also have at least three years of full-time work experience.

In addition, candidates must be between twenty-three and thirty-five years old, willing to accept assignment anywhere in the United States, and be in excellent physical condition, with at least 20/200 vision corrected to 20/40 in one eye and 20/20 in the other. All new agents undergo fifteen weeks of training at the FBI Academy at the U.S. Marine Corps Base in Quantico, Virginia.

Applicants for special agent jobs with the U.S. Treasury Department must have a college degree or minimum of three years of work experience, at least two of which are in criminal investigation, or a comparable combination of experience and education. Candidates must be in excellent physical condition and be less than thirty-five years old at the time they begin duty. Treasury agents undergo eight weeks of training at the Federal Law Enforcement Training Center in Glenco, Georgia, plus eight weeks of specialized training with the particular bureau.

Your Future in Law Enforcement

We've become a more security-conscious society in the aftermath of the terrorist attack on America in 2001. Because of that, employment in law enforcement is expected to grow at a faster-than-average rate.

Still, competition will be extremely keen for special-agent positions with the FBI, U.S. Treasury Department, and other federal homeland security agencies. These are prestigious jobs in law enforcement and tend to attract more applicants than there are openings. Consequently, only the most highly qualified candidates will win these jobs.

Police and special agents usually work forty-hour weeks. On the other hand, because the services of their agencies are provided around the clock, some officers work weekends, holidays, and nights. Since police and special agents can be called to duty at any time their services are needed, they may have to work overtime, particularly during complex criminal investigations.

And, of course, the jobs of some special agents, such as those on the Secret Service's presidential squad, require extensive and far-flung travel.

Uniformed police officers, plainclothes detectives, and special agents may have to work outdoors for long periods in all kinds of weather. The injury rate among them is higher than in many other occupations, largely because of the risks involved in pursuing speeding motorists, apprehending dangerous criminals, and dealing with public disorders.

Earnings and Benefits

Annual salaries of police officers range from $30,460 to $58,900, with a median of $39,790. The median for police and detective supervisors is $57,210, and the highest-paid 10 percent earn about $86,060. The median salary for federal agents is $70,070; for state officers, $53,960. Federal law enforcement officers usually receive extra pay because of the major amount of overtime they work.

For More Information

If you are interested in becoming a local or state police officer, contact your local and state police department and civil service commission.

Federal Bureau of Investigation
935 Pennsylvania Avenue NW
Washington, DC 20535
www.fbi.gov
   (Call local or state FBI offices listed in your local phone directory.)

U.S. Marshals Service
Human Resources Division
Law Enforcement Recruiting
Washington, DC 20530
www.usdoj.gov/marshals

U.S. Secret Service
Personnel Division
950 H Street NW, Suite 912
Washington, DC 20223
www.treas.gov/usss

U.S. Bureau of Alcohol, Tobacco, and Firearms
Personnel Division
650 Massachusetts Avenue NW, Room 4100
Washington, DC 20226
www.atf.treas.gov

Pamphlets with general information about jobs as special agents with these and other federal agencies are available from any U.S. Office of Personnel Management Job Information Center (listed in phone directories under U.S. Government, Office of Personnel Management) and at www.usajobs.opm.gov.

CHAPTER SEVEN

Representing the United States Abroad

Peace Corps Volunteers

Since President John F. Kennedy created the Peace Corps in 1961, American volunteers have been sharing their skills and energy with people in the poorer areas of the world—the so-called developing countries. The Peace Corps mission is to promote world peace and friendship by helping the people of interested countries meet their needs for trained men and women and by encouraging mutual understanding between people in the United States and those in the countries the Peace Corps serves.

At the invitation of host governments, about sixty five hundred Peace Corps volunteers now serve in ninety countries. The Peace Corps is the only U.S. government agency that places its people in communities to live and work directly with the people of developing nations.

Peace Corps volunteers have made many friends for the United States by demonstrating that they personally care about their host country communities—care enough to spend two years of their lives working directly with the people to make life better. They provide assistance in education, health and nutrition, agriculture, forestry and environment, engineering, industrial arts, and business development.

As a Peace Corps volunteer, you will travel primarily to the underdeveloped areas of the world. And during your service, usually two years, you are encouraged to use your vacation time to further explore the country where you are stationed.

The Work of the Peace Corps

Peace Corps volunteers work side by side with host-country coworkers to make things happen—useful, appropriate, and lasting things. The projects they work on are determined by the communities where volunteers are stationed. The Peace Corps volunteer's mission is not to do things for people, but to help people do things for themselves.

For example, volunteers are teaching farmers in several African countries how to cultivate tilapia, a fish that tolerates bad water, consumes insects and agricultural byproducts, and reproduces every three months. Tilapia is a rich source of protein. African farmers who recognize its value can pass the technology on to other generations by instructing their children in the cultivation of tilapia.

Peace Corps volunteers helped the people of Mali establish a local soap-making factory, where villagers can earn cash incomes. In Nepal, a volunteer at a school for the deaf has helped develop the first sign-language dictionary in Nepali. Volunteers have introduced science and business curricula in the Kingdom of Tonga, shown Paraguayan farmers how to stop soil erosion, taught Ghanaian students masonry techniques, designed water supply systems in Belize, and helped develop disease-resistant vegetables in Western Samoa.

Before serving in the Peace Corps, many would-be volunteers think that physical hardship will be the most difficult part of the experience. In hindsight, however, most of them see things differently. The most common difficulty they report is adapting to the slow pace at which change occurs. Many volunteers see a huge gap between the existing situation and the potential for transforming it. To bring about change that will remain after the volunteer returns home may be the most challenging and motivating aspect of Peace Corps service.

Says one Peace Corps veteran, "I would and have advised other people, including my mother, to join the Peace Corps. I wouldn't, however, advise everyone to join because the experience is not for everyone. I believe you have to be adventurous, very adaptable, and really want to be where you are," says this volunteer. "The most difficult part for me has been being apart from family and friends."

But another returned worker says, "I intend to join the Peace Corps again after I retire. I fell in love, I fell sick, I fell off my mule (twice), and, most of all, I fell for my town. Peace Corps gives you a healthy dose of how the majority of people in the world live."

Most Peace Corps assignments are for two years and begin after the completion of training. Vacation time is accrued at two days per month, and volunteers are encouraged to use it for travel in the host country.

Training sessions usually take between eight and twelve weeks and are most often held in the host countries. Volunteers are expected to speak the language of the people with whom they live and work, so language instruction is intense during this period. Instructors are host-country nationals, often with years of experience working with Peace Corps volunteers. The training includes in-depth orientation to the culture and traditions of the host country and technical instruction to help you adapt your skills to your particular overseas assignments.

Volunteers work for a government department, agency, or organization in the host country. They are supervised by, and work with, host-country nationals, and they are subject to local laws.

Getting into the Peace Corps

Any healthy adult U.S. citizen is eligible to apply for the Peace Corps. Married couples are welcome if both can work and are qualified to be volunteers. Blacks and other minorities are especially sought for Peace Corps assignments, and older persons are also welcome. Although fewer than 10 percent of Peace Corps volunteers are fifty years old and older, host-country governments say they want more older Americans as volunteers. Many societies overseas place high value on age and associate it with wisdom.

For many assignments, knowledge of a language other than English is necessary. Previous fluency in that language can be very helpful but is not always required because of the intensive language instruction provided in Peace Corps training.

To be accepted to a Peace Corps assignment, your skills must match the criteria requested by host countries for particular programs. These criteria vary with different areas. Most require a four-year college degree and often three to five years of relevant work experience or a master's degree. Selection from among liberal arts graduates is highly competitive. Community service and your character and personality are also factors in selection. The Peace Corps looks for people with perseverance, adaptability, creativity in problem solving, and sociability.

Specialties generally in demand include agriculturalists, natural resources managers, and teacher trainers. Liberal arts generalists are welcome and can help on projects as diverse as fish farming, beekeeping, health and nutrition, community services, and general leadership and organizing. Fishery specialists, engineers, businesspeople (especially those who can help developers of small business enterprises and cooperatives), nurses and other health professionals, home economists, skilled tradespeople, and educators are also encouraged to volunteer.

Apply to join the Peace Corps at least nine months prior to the time you'll be available. The application process can take up to a year, but you must be ready to begin service within one year of submitting application forms. In some cases, it is possible to start training as early as three months after your application is received. Selection for an assignment comes only after you have been invited to enter a training program and successfully completed it.

Life in the Peace Corps

Most Peace Corps assignments last two years, beginning after your completion of training. Volunteers may request an extension of service in order to complete a particular project or activity. Extensions must be approved by the country director.

During your two years, all expenses related to your service—travel, health care and insurance, housing, vacation (forty-five days during the two years), and monthly living expenses (paid in the local currency for food, clothing, household, and incidental expenses)—are provided by the Peace Corps.

In the Peace Corps, you receive full health benefits. Trainees must pass rigorous medical examinations and receive immunizations and health training before they leave the United States, and they will not be sent to countries where their health needs cannot be met.

The Peace Corps maintains a medical staff in most countries. Where there is not a staff, local health professionals are fully trained, and there are facilities equipped to handle emergencies. If medical problems occur that cannot be treated locally, the volunteer is sent to a modern facility in another country or back to the United States.

Every effort is made to ensure the safety of Peace Corps volunteers. Each Peace Corps post overseas has an emergency plan for coping with natural disasters or other threats to volunteers' health and well-being.

Can you choose where you want to serve? Possibly. The application form allows you to indicate area preferences as well as those places where you do not wish to serve. You will not be assigned to a country or region where you do not want to go. To be sent to a particular country, however, a volunteer must have a skill currently being requested by that country. If you are only willing to serve in one country or area, your chances of being accepted are limited. Personal flexibility with regard to assignments is very important to help the Peace Corps fill the requests of many host countries.

In most locations, you will work in collaboration with a host-country national assigned to the same project. Another Peace Corps volunteer may be posted in a nearby village or town. In larger urban areas, of course, a number of Peace Corps volunteers working on a variety of projects may reside in the same area.

Living situations vary enormously from one country to another and depend on the nature of the program. Many volunteers live in cement, brick, or adobe houses. Generally the more rural the program, the more basic the housing will be. In urban areas, volunteers' quarters often have running water and electricity. Most volunteers live comfortably but very modestly.

Your Future in the Peace Corps

Your future as a Peace Corps volunteer is mostly beyond your service in the corps. When Peace Corps volunteers return home, their experience can help shape their future. The benefits of two years in the Peace Corps include great personal growth, a new perspective on the world, travel, and a greater understanding of how the United States is perceived by other cultures.

There are also specific career benefits: language and skills training, hands-on experience in the developing world, and some specially created career and educational opportunities. For instance, more than fifty institutions offer scholarships and assistantships for returned volunteers. In some states, overseas teaching experience may be substituted for practice teaching requirements necessary for professional accreditation as a teacher. Volunteers receive a $5,400 readjustment allowance at the end of their tours and are eligible for federal employment on a noncompetitive basis. Also, the Peace Corps Fellows/USA program can open doors for returned volunteers seeking education and career help.

Says a Peace Corps veteran: "I could come up with a long list of ex-volunteers scattered among banking, finance, international trade, and development agencies who are reaching midlevel and, in some cases, senior positions. When you put us all together, we're becoming a pretty influential group, particularly in regard to Africa and other developing regions."

For More Information

Peace Corps
The Paul D. Coverdell Peace Corps Headquarters
1111 Twentieth Street NW
Washington, DC 20526
www.peacecorps.gov

. . . .

Foreign Service Officers

The very title, Foreign Service Officer, conjures exotic images of travel to faraway places. For those travel buffs who relish international travel, this could be the career for you. Being a part of the Foreign Service is certainly a career field where travel and living in foreign destinations is a routine part of your work.

A career in the Foreign Service is more than just a job. It is a way of life that requires a special commitment to representing the United States to the people of other countries.

Like any occupation, a Foreign Service career can bring hardships and challenges, but it can also bring you excitement, glamour, unique rewards, and exceptional professional and personal opportunities. Additionally, you'll have the personal satisfaction of serving your country and representing America's interests—and caring for the needs of American citizens—in other countries around the world.

There are two types of career paths in the Foreign Service. Foreign Service Officers (FSOs) are generalists who perform administrative, consular, economic, and political functions. Foreign Service Specialists perform technical, support, and special administrative services. Employees on both tracks work at embassies and posts around the world as well as in Washington, D.C.

FSOs might experience the glamour of dining with the ambassador as guests in a Middle Eastern palace or the excitement of being involved in preparations for a summit meeting of international heads of state. But for the most part, the day-to-day routine of the FSO is much like that of other white-collar managers and administrators. The significant difference between work in the Foreign Service and that in other branches of government is the location.

The FSO may work in lively western European or Asian capitals, in the hostile climate of Antarctica, or in a remote refugee camp in a developing country. Many overseas posts are in remote locations where harsh climates and health hazards prevail and where American-style amenities may be hard to come by. Service at some posts may entail security risks for FSOs and their families.

That's why a decision to join the Foreign Service requires unusual motivation and a firm dedication to serve the public and defend and advance U.S. interests abroad. The Foreign Service officer can help shape U.S. policy by providing accurate analysis and advice based on experience and by providing dissenting views when warranted.

At the same time, FSOs must accept political and policy direction from the president's administration and direct their efforts to making those policies succeed. In a field as potentially controversial as foreign affairs, the professional Foreign Service officer is expected to place loyalty and willingness to follow instructions above personal opinions and preferences.

In many ways, FSOs are to foreign affairs what military officers are to defense. FSOs work closely with members of the civil and military services and take their policy instructions from political appointees. They can be sent anywhere in the world, at any time, to serve the diplomatic needs of the United States. They are truly the front line personnel of all U.S. embassies, consulates, and other diplomatic missions and may also be assigned to other civilian and military agencies to help them carry out their foreign policy missions.

In general, Foreign Service employees are rotated to new assignments every two to four years. During their careers, they'll live overseas about 60 percent of the time. The government covers the expense of spouses, children under twenty-one, and dependent parents who wish to accompany an FSO to foreign posts in most circumstances. Security concerns and the lack of adequate educational or health facilities at some posts may deter families from accompanying Foreign Service employees to some overseas posts.

The Work of the Foreign Service

In addition to its embassies in other national capitals, the United States maintains consulates general or consulates in many other foreign cities. These are the branch offices of embassies. Primarily responsible for serving and protecting the millions of Americans who live, work, and travel abroad, these consular posts issue visas and passports and provide the embassy with political and economic reporting from the region. In all, the U.S. State Department operates more than 250 posts overseas.

For many years, FSOs were viewed as generalists who, like career military officers, were assigned to various jobs in different parts of the world throughout their careers. Most FSOs still are generalists. Yet, just as the military is now attracting a new breed of officers who are more likely to be specialists, the Foreign Service is seeking candidates interested in more than political science or diplomatic history. Transnational issues characterize diplomacy now. Among these issues are science and technology (including the global fight against diseases such as AIDS and efforts to save the environment), antinarcotics and antiterrorism efforts, and international trade. So the Foreign Service seeks officers who can specialize in dealing with U.S. diplomacy in these areas.

Duties of Foreign Service Officers

There are several kinds of work that foreign service officers do in posts around the world:

Administration. FSOs are responsible for all support operations of an overseas post—hiring foreign national personnel, assuring reliable communications with Washington, overseeing sophisticated computer systems, managing the post's financial operations, providing office and residential space, and assuring the best possible security for the post's personnel and property. Competent administration is critically important, especially in hostile areas.

Consular Services. In solving the vast range of human problems they encounter every day, consular services employees need the combined skills of social worker, lawyer, judge, and investigator. Consular functions range from the mundane—issuing passports, visas, and federal benefits payments—to the extraordinary, such as finding a lost traveler or investigating the safety of a child involved in a custody dispute.

Economic Analysis. The economic analysts at embassies and consular posts deal with matters ranging from commercial aviation safety, fishing rights, and international lending practices to scientific cooperation and the environmental impact of economic development. From their contact with key foreign business and financial leaders, these FSOs prepare reports on local economic conditions and their impact on American trade and investment policies.

Political Affairs. Political analysis and reporting on the views of political opponents, as well as foreign government officials, are necessary to assess the impact of U.S. policies in other countries. Political affairs FSOs cultivate contacts among labor unions, social and humanitarian organizations, local educators, and cultural leaders, all of whom may provide clues to future domestic and foreign policy shifts in the host country.

Information and Cultural Affairs. FSOs in information services departments manage cultural, informational, and public diplomacy programs at U.S. posts overseas. For example, a USIA information officer might arrange briefings, interviews, press conferences, and other media activities to boost understanding and support for U.S. programs. A cultural affairs officer administers educational exchange programs and coordinates U.S. cultural and sports presentations.

Commercial and Business Services. FSOs working for the U.S. and Foreign Commercial Service (FCS) of the Department of Commerce identify overseas business connections for American exporters and investors, conduct market research for American products, and organize trade promotion events. These officers combine the imagination of an entrepreneur with the skills of an analyst and a broker to enhance opportunities for American trade across the seas.

The Foreign Service needs qualified men and women who want to serve their country in this capacity. The service especially seeks persons from varied ethnic and racial backgrounds from all regions of the United States to reflect the great diversity of the American people. Salaries are comparable to those of other federal government employees in similar job areas. Entering FSOs start at junior grades FS-5 and FS-6, with starting salaries between $25,011 and $27,878, depending on education and experience.

Foreign Service salaries may be enhanced by such benefits as the shipment of household furnishings and cars to overseas posts; travel and lodging payments en route; government-provided housing, furniture, and utilities overseas; home leave (including travel expenses); and medical benefits. There are also education and travel allowances for dependent children, cost-of-living allowances to help cover extra expenses in high-cost foreign cities, and special pay for danger and hardship posts.

Foreign Service Specialists
Foreign Service specialists work at the same posts as FSOs around the world. They deal with a wide variety of functions, ranging

from financial, information, telecommunications, and personnel management to security, medical, and secretarial operations. Their job descriptions and pay scales are as follows.

General Services Officers. These specialists manage physical resources and logistical functions at Foreign Service posts, everything from procurement of supplies to transportation and building maintenance. Salary range: $43,934 to $64,519.

Financial Management Officers. These officers work on the financial operations of overseas posts. Salary range: $43,934 to $64,519.

Human Resources Officers. The Foreign Service employs people to manage personnel services at overseas posts. Salary range: $43,934 to $64,519.

Office Management Specialists. The Foreign Service always needs people to perform secretarial and related duties. Salary range: $28,450 to $41,780.

Regional Medical Officers, RMO/Psychiatrists, and Health Practitioners. These officers provide health care to U.S. government employees and dependents, evaluate local medical care facilities and advise on local community health problems, and arrange for emergency medical evacuations. Also supporting the medical program are medical technologists and nurse practitioners. Salary range: regional medical officers, $82,580 to $107,357; health practitioners, $54,220 to $79,624.

Information Management Specialists and Technical Specialists. This job involves handling operation and maintenance of communications equipment (radio, telephone, and digital communications) at diplomatic and consular posts. Salary range: $35,819 to $52,278.

Diplomatic Security Officers. They are responsible for the security of U.S. facilities, operations, and personnel abroad. They perform investigative and protective work to deal with criminal, intelligence, and terrorist activities that might threaten American lives and property. Salary range: $33,763 to $46,736.

Security Engineering Officers. These officers conduct technical security surveys and inspections and maintain security equipment used at diplomatic and consular posts. Salary range: $41,292 to $60,639.

Facilities Maintenance Specialists. They are highly skilled managers responsible for the maintenance and repair of U.S. government-owned and government-leased property abroad. Salary range: $50,932 to $64,519.

Construction Engineers. They supervise contractors to ensure proper building of new properties or improvements to existing ones. Salary range: $35,599 to $64,519.

Facilities Maintenance Technicians. These technicians provide facilities maintenance such as electrical power and heating, ventilating and air conditioning. Salary range: $50,932 to $64,519.

Getting into the Foreign Service

Applicants for FSO and specialist positions must be U.S. citizens, be at least twenty-one years old at the time of employment, pass a medical exam, have an appropriate educational background for the position (from a high school diploma to university degrees and professional licenses), and be available for assignment anywhere in the world.

Openings for specialists are listed and described in vacancy announcements, which you can request from the federal Office of Personnel Management (OPM). The announcements note specific job requirements. The process of applying for a job can take from six months to a year. Your completed application is reviewed by a screening panel. If you pass this review, you'll be invited to an interview, usually in Washington, D.C. If you pass the interview stage, you'll be subject to a thorough background investigation. You'll also be required to take a pre-employment drug-screening exam. (Once hired, all Foreign Service employees are subject to random drug testing.)

The purpose of the background investigation is to determine your eligibility for a security clearance as well as your general suitability for the Foreign Service. The investigation covers such matters as registration for Selective Service, repayment of federally guaranteed student loans, credit and tax history, employment records, and drug or alcohol abuse. Investigators may interview your current and previous employers, coworkers, contacts, and neighbors. Depending on your work history, places of residence, and travels, the background check can take several months.

If you get through these initial stages and you are applying for a specialist job, your name will be placed on a register for a maximum of eighteen months. Candidates for jobs are hired from the register as openings become available.

The entry screening process for Foreign Service officers includes a written examination as well as an interview assessment. Success on both of these requires a strong command of English.

Although no specific educational background is stipulated, most successful FSO candidates have at least a bachelor's degree and a broad knowledge of international and domestic political affairs, U.S. and world history, government and foreign policy, and culture. In recent years, about 65 percent of FSO candidates had advanced degrees in international relations, economics, business administration, law, journalism, or other disciplines. Many have had work experience in various fields before their appointments.

Before accepting any Foreign Service job, you must agree to be available for assignment worldwide. Factors that will determine where you'll be sent include the need at a particular post for certain skills and specializations as well as personal preferences. Medical clearance for overseas duty is required for candidates and their dependents.

Your Future in the Foreign Service

FSO applicants who pass the initial tests and assessments and receive security and medical clearances can be hired as FSO career candidates. During a five-year probationary period, they'll be reviewed for tenure and commissioning as Foreign Service officers, usually by the fourth year. A probationary candidate who fails to perform satisfactorily during this period can be fired.

When hired for a Foreign Service specialist job, applicants become career candidates for a probationary period not to exceed four years. During that time they will be considered for tenure; if they don't make it on the first review, they'll have another chance twelve months later. If they don't get tenure then, they'll have to leave the Foreign Service.

When you enter the Foreign Service, you receive several weeks of basic training in Washington, D.C., at the State Department's Foreign Service Institute. Initial training usually includes orientation to the Foreign Service, study about the area where you're to be posted, training in your job field, and some foreign language study. For some Foreign Service employees, the training can take up to seven months prior to the first overseas assignment, most of it involving language instruction.

Entering FSOs who already are professionally competent in a foreign language may get through this part of the training in relatively short order. It is not absolutely necessary that you know a foreign language when you apply for the Foreign Service. At the same time, if you have a demonstrated aptitude in learning foreign languages, that will be a plus for you, as all FSOs must learn a foreign language before they receive tenure in the service.

Most Foreign Service career candidates will be assigned abroad following their training in Washington. They should expect to serve a minimum of one year performing consular work some time during their first two tours of duty. Subsequent assignments will depend on their interests and functional specialization and the needs of the service.

For More Information

Recruitment Division
U.S. Department of State
2201 C Street NW
Washington, DC 20520
www.state.gov

U.S. Office of Personnel Management
1900 E Street NW
Washington, DC 20415
www.usajobs.opm.gov

U.S. Agency for International Development
Information Center
Ronald Reagan Building
Washington, DC 20523
www.usaid.gov

Information Services (SXCI)
Department of Foreign Affairs
International Trade
125 Sussex Drive
Ottawa, ON K1A 0G2
Canada
www.dfait-maeci.gc.ca

CHAPTER EIGHT

Rock Stars, Movie Stars, and Space Travelers

In this chapter is an assortment of jobs that bring with them plenty of cross-country and round-the-world travel. While there are not large numbers of them, maybe you have that special talent needed to catapult yourself to fame. You may discover you're just the person to be a traveling superstar!

Musicians and Dancers

Of professional entertainers, the ones we most often think of as travelers are the musical performers. Even in a world of tapes, CDs, and other recorded forms of music, musicians take to the road to present themselves to audiences in every nook and cranny of the country. Nothing beats live performances.

For big rock bands, major concert tours are often an annual event. A new album release may kick off a cross-country or world tour, and another album may result from recordings during live concerts. Country-western bands spend so much time on the road that many have their own customized buses. Willie Nelson's "On the Road Again" is the anthem of country bands. Even symphony orchestras tour to other cities. And when musicians travel, they usually take their bands, backup singers, dancers, warm-up bands, and technicians such as lighting and sound experts.

The Musician's Life

Look around. Listen. Almost every kind of music is available to you on the radio and in recordings—rock, country-western, gospel, classical, pop, rhythm and blues, jazz, heavy metal, zydeco, salsa, reggae, and hip hop. There is a vast audience for music of all kinds. In every city and hamlet, you can usually find places to listen to live music.

Singers and instrumental musicians generally work nights and weekends. That's when most performances are held. When they're not on stage, of course, musicians spend a lot of time practicing. Many musicians earn money from their music only on a part-time basis (about 40 percent, and another 40 are self-employed). So they may have to squeeze rehearsal time in between nonmusical jobs from which they really earn a living. The timeworn expression in this profession is, "Don't quit your day job."

The top traveling bands and musical groups usually work out of the major entertainment and recording centers—New York, Los Angeles, Nashville, and Detroit. There are more than sixteen hundred professional orchestras and small chamber music groups in the United States, and many of these groups also travel for part of the year.

Some musicians' road trips can be a real grind, like the classic one-night gigs in one-horse towns: The bus pulls into town several hours before a performance. The musicians scramble to freshen up and practice. An hour after the last encore, they're back in the bus on the way to the next town circled on the map. That's certainly no way to appreciate your travels.

But other musical groups travel on a saner schedule. They may spend several days or a week in cities on their itinerary, with time for sightseeing and sampling local restaurants. Musicians, dancers, and other variety entertainers also take occasional bookings on cruise ships that travel the Caribbean, Mexico's Pacific coast, Hawaii, and the Mediterranean. During the day, these entertainers may get to recreate ashore.

Getting into the Business

Musicians and dancers usually begin working when they are very young, and their success will depend to a great extent on their natural talent. Their greatest desires are to perform before audiences, to be seen and heard, and hopefully to become a star.

Musicians also find paying jobs in musical shows at major entertainment complexes, such as Walt Disney World in Florida and Disneyland in California, the Grand Old Opry in Nashville, and Busch Gardens, Six Flags and Paramount theme parks around the country. Regional influences are strong in American music, and in addition to the major music-industry centers noted, recording studios and related music businesses also draw musicians to cities such as Miami, Las Vegas, New Orleans, Memphis, and Branson, Missouri.

Opportunities for musicians will grow at an average pace. Most new jobs probably will be in the religious music field.

In show business, of course, a performer's earnings ultimately depend on the size, ardor, and loyalty of the audience—their star power. Among journeymen performers, the median annual salary of employed musicians, singers, and dancers is $36,740. The highest-paid 10 percent earn $88,640 or more. In symphony orchestras, salaries typically range from $24,720 to $100,196. A typical season for top orchestras can be anywhere from forty-seven to fifty-two weeks. Earnings in all of these jobs often depend on the number of hours and weeks worked. Most of these entertainers belong to the American Federation of Musicians of the U.S. and Canada, the American Guild of Musical Artists, or other unions, which establish minimum wage scales.

Of course, the most successful musicians earn performance and recording fees that far exceed these median and typical amounts. Indeed, like TV and movie stars, the top musicians earn money in the millions. Star singers and instrumentalists often perform a song or two on a TV show more for publicity and exposure than for the union scale wages these shows pay.

For More Information

American Federation of Musicians of the United States
    and Canada
1501 Broadway, Suite 600
New York, NY 10036
www.afm.org

American Guild of Musical Artists
1430 Broadway, Fourteenth Floor
New York, NY 10018
www.musicalartists.org

American Symphony Orchestra League
New York Headquarters
33 West Sixtieth Street, Fifth Floor
New York, NY 10023
www.symphony.org

American Symphony Orchestra League
Washington Office
910 Seventeenth Street NW
Washington, DC 20006

National Association of Schools of Music
11250 Roger Bacon Drive, Suite 21
Reston, VA 20190
www.arts-accredit.org

National Dance Association
The American Alliance for Health, Physical Education,
    Recreation, and Dance
1900 Association Drive
Reston, VA 20191
www.aahperd.org/nda/template.cfm

American Dance Guild
P.O. Box 2006
Lennox Hill Station
New York, NY 10021
www.americandanceguild.org

....

Stage, Film, and Television Actors

Touring companies of actors and stage technicians are a tradition of the theater. Performers with popular shows can easily spend the better part of a year on the road. Motion picture actors also spend a lot of time traveling.

Movies aren't just a Hollywood industry anymore. In the first half of the previous century, most movies were made totally on Hollywood sound stages—huge buildings the size of aircraft hangars, where scenes of offices, homes, factory floors, city streets, and even jungles and mountaintops can be replicated for scenes in movies. Now major motion picture producers tend to use the magic of computer graphics or to look for the real thing as a backdrop, no matter where on Earth it is.

More and more nowadays, moviemakers take to the road in the quest for locations for their films. You'll find movies being made in little towns in North Carolina and Louisiana, on the streets of Chicago, New York, Toronto, Vancouver, and other major U.S. and Canadian cities.

Motion picture assistance offices in many states, provinces, and cities offer cost incentives to attract filmmakers to their locations. Making a movie can bring jobs to local actors and would-be actors who might get roles as "extras," and it brings business to local carpenters, rental equipment companies, restaurants and caterers, hotels, and other firms.

Even movies filmed in Hollywood shoot scenes on locations all around the Los Angeles area. A tour company in Hollywood sells maps and schedules of location shooting by film companies every day in Southern California, so movie fans can watch movies being made and maybe catch a glimpse of a star.

So, actors, directors, producers, cinematographers, and the dozens of other kinds of workers involved in the production of movies and stage plays are frequent travelers. Read the fan magazines and entertainment columns for their itineraries—Ben Affleck and Morgan Freeman are in Baltimore and Washington to film a spy thriller. Brad Pitt and Julia Roberts are filming in Mexico. Nathan Lane is traveling to London with the stage show "The Producers." Actors are off to Africa or Italy or wherever the scenery fits the movie script—and to theater stages in hundreds of communities across the United States.

How and Where Actors Work

Acting requires persistence, practice, and hard work, as well as special talent. Only a handful of actors achieve recognition as stars on stage and screen. A somewhat larger number of actors are well known, experienced performers who frequently appear in movies, plays, and television productions.

But most actors struggle for even a toehold in this profession, picking up parts wherever they can get them. It's an unsteady career; the majority of actors experience frequent periods of unemployment. Many hold day jobs as waiters, salespeople, or file clerks so they can make time to go to casting calls and make the rounds in pursuit of acting jobs. Some actors teach acting courses in schools and community workshops.

Beginning actors usually start in bit parts with just a few speaking lines in school and local and regional theater productions. They hope critics, agents, and producers will hear of them and call with offers of larger supporting roles. In the theater, rookie actors may serve as understudies for the principal actors in a play. They actually play the role if the principal is sick or must be away from the production for a day or two. In film and television, actors may hope to move from roles in commercials to movies or TV series. Successful, versatile actors who can manage to play a variety of roles in movie and stage productions usually stay busy.

Actors work at odd hours. Plays are performed mostly in the evenings. Filming for movies or TV shows may begin early in the morning and go on well into the night, especially when the crew is at a special location, where the work must be done while the light and weather and other circumstances are right for the scene.

Good performances by actors require memorizing lines and many rehearsals of action. It takes physical stamina to stand the heat of stage and studio lights and endure the long, irregular hours and adverse weather or living conditions that may exist on location. But oh, the chance to be a star!

Some actors eventually become directors. Directors show and tell actors how they should interpret plays or scripts. Directors can become as famous as the stars they direct. Nearly every movie fan knows who Steven Spielberg is. Director George Lucas is a cult figure to fans of his *Star Wars* films. The late David Lean was known worldwide for the sprawling, dramatic landscapes in his classic films *Lawrence of Arabia, Bridge on the River Kwai,* and *Doctor Zhivago.*

Directors usually are in charge of the entire cast and crew on a movie or stage production. They conduct auditions and rehearsals and select cast members. They usually approve scenery and costumes, music and choreography. They use their knowledge of acting and the medium in which they are working to pull the best possible performances from their actors.

Getting into the Business

Actors usually try to get into the business at an early age. They get the acting bug while performing in high school or college plays or summer theater and keep plugging away to make it to the big time. To gain experience, they may seek every opportunity to work in local theater groups and in dinner theater productions, where they wait tables during intermissions. To hone their acting skills, they may take formal training at dramatic arts schools in New York or Los Angeles or at colleges and universities around the country.

Some directors come to this occupation from long careers as successful actors. Others come directly from film craft university programs, primarily in California and New York. Would-be directors who have a bachelor's degree or two years of on-the-set experience in motion picture or television production may qualify for the assistant directors training program of the Directors Guild of America and cooperating movie and television companies. To qualify, you must take a written test and go through a series of group and individual assessments. Of the thousand or so applicants every year, only eight to fifteen are selected.

For most actors and directors, career advancement comes with a growing reputation for success—artistic and at the box office. Actors and directors whose work can assure that a play or movie will make money are besieged with offers of bigger and better roles and movie projects.

Your Future in Acting

Jobs for actors and technicians in the industry are expected to grow faster than average in the years ahead because the number of theatrical, motion picture, and television productions should continue to grow. This growth will be fueled by rising foreign demand for American productions and expanding domestic demand from the cable television, home movie rental, and TV syndication sectors of the industry, as well as more productions from independent filmmakers, a vibrant regional theatre network, and development of interactive media for the Internet.

The market for live stage productions will continue to be strong in the future, as many people prefer live theater for its immediacy and aesthetics. Attendance at live theater performances will continue to increase as regional and touring shows reach audiences in more and more cities outside the traditional center of theater in New York City.

With an enormous variety of programming on television, actors are employed not only as players in dramas and sitcoms, but as hosts, hostesses, guides, moderators, and narrators for TV productions—documentaries, "reality" shows in which "real people" participate, and exploration and adventure features.

That's the good news. The bad news for actors is that with the always-huge number of people who want to be stars and the lack of formal entry procedures and requirements, competition for acting and directing jobs is fierce. Only the most talented and tenacious will be able to grab the brass ring and find steady employment in show business.

For those who do, the rewards can be modest, or they may be stratospheric. Because they work so irregularly, many actors earn minimal amounts from the craft in the course of a year. Still, annual earnings for actors range from $16,950 to $59,769, with the highest-paid 10 percent making $93,620 or more.

Most show business workers belong to guilds or unions that negotiate minimum wage scales with production companies. The Actors' Equity Association represents stage actors; the Screen Actors Guild and Screen Extras Guild represent actors in movies, television, and commercials; the American Federation of Television and Radio Artists (AFTRA) represents performers in these media. Most stage directors belong to the Society of Stage Directors and Choreographers; film and TV directors belong to the Directors Guild of America.

The minimum union wage for actors in Broadway productions is $1,252 a week; in small off-Broadway theaters, it is $440 to $551 a week. Actors on the road in companies of stage shows can add $106 a day for living expenses. Eight performances comprise a week's work on the stage, and additional performances bring overtime pay. Actors may work long hours during rehearsals, but once the show opens, they work more regular hours, about twenty-four hours a week. The Guild minimum wage for motion picture and television actors with speaking parts is $636 a day, or $2,206 for a five-day week. TV actors also receive additional compensation for reruns of their shows.

Of course, through their agents, successful actors and directors negotiate deals with movie, TV, and theatrical production companies for payments that far surpass union-negotiated wages.

For More Information

Actors' Equity Association
165 West Forty-Sixth Street
New York, NY 10036
www.actorsequity.org

Canadian Actors' Equity Association
44 Victoria Street, Twelfth Floor
Toronto, ON M5C 3C4
Canada
www.caea.com

Screen Actors Guild
5757 Wilshire Boulevard
Los Angeles, CA 90036
www.sag.org

American Federation of Television and Radio Artists
National Office—New York
260 Madison Avenue
New York, NY 10016
www.aftra.org

American Federation of Television and Radio Artists
National Office—Los Angeles
5757 Wilshire Boulevard, Ninth Floor
Los Angeles, CA 90036

Directors Guild of America
7920 Sunset Boulevard
Los Angeles, CA 90046
www.dga.org

American Guild of Variety Artists
184 Fifth Avenue, Sixth Floor
New York, NY 10010

National Association of Schools of Theater
11250 Roger Bacon Drive, Suite 21
Reston, VA 20190
www.arts-accredit.org

. . . .

Astronauts

The twenty-first century promises the reality of humans living
and working in space. The United States and its international
partners Canada, Japan, Russia, and the European Space Agency
operate the International Space Station. From this orbiting depot,
humans may eventually continue their journeys to other planets.
Talk about travel! Some of the trips proposed for future astronauts
may take years to complete.

The specifics have yet to be worked out, but by comparison
these efforts could dwarf the Apollo program, which first sent
astronauts to the moon. Perhaps a lunar base will be established,
where in addition to making forays themselves, astronauts will
control an army of versatile robotic workers and explorers. Mean-
while, automated spacecraft will continue to probe Mars to gauge
the potential for human visitation in the future.

In seeking astronauts for the first U.S. manned space flight in
1961, the National Aeronautics and Space Administration (NASA)
required jet aircraft flight experience and engineering training.
Astronauts could be no more than five feet eleven inches tall

because of limited cabin space in the Mercury space capsule then being designed.

As America's first astronauts, NASA selected seven men from an original field of five hundred candidates. They have become almost legendary figures: Scott Carpenter, Gordon Cooper, Gus Grissom, Deke Slayton, John Glenn, Wally Schirra, and Alan Shepard.

In 1962, nine more pilot astronauts were chosen; in 1963, fourteen more. Then, in 1964, the first six scientist astronauts were selected. They were chosen on the basis of educational background alone—each of them had a doctorate or equivalent experience in the natural sciences, medicine, or engineering. NASA chose nineteen more pilot astronauts in 1966 and eleven more scientist astronauts in 1967.

Those who stand out in the astronaut corps, beyond the original seven, are Neil Armstrong, Buzz Aldrin, and Michael Collins, who flew the first moon-landing mission. Armstrong and Aldrin were the first to walk on the moon, while Collins controlled the spaceship that would return the three astronauts to Earth.

By 1978, the first group of astronaut candidates for the space shuttle program were selected. There were twenty mission specialists and fifteen pilots who completed training and became active-status astronauts in that class. Six of them were women, and four were members of minorities. Additional groups of pilots and mission specialists were added to the astronaut corps through the 1980s.

Training for Space Travel

Astronaut candidates receive training at the Johnson Space Center near Houston, Texas. They attend classes in basic science and technology, including mathematics, Earth resources, meteorology, guidance and navigation, astronomy, physics, and computers. Candidates also receive training in the use of space tools, space suits, parachute jumping, and land and sea survival procedures.

They are exposed to problems associated with high (hyperbaric) and low (hypobaric) atmospheric pressures in altitude chambers. They also experience the microgravity of space flight; this weightlessness is achieved in thirty-second periods as a large jet airplane dives from thirty-four thousand feet to twenty-four thousand feet dozens of times in a day. Pilot astronauts maintain their flying proficiency by flying at least fifteen hours a month in NASA trainer jets.

The astronauts begin their formal space transportation system training by reading manuals and by taking computer-based training lessons on the various space orbiter systems. Next, they work in the single systems trainer, where each astronaut is accompanied by an instructor who helps him or her learn about the operations of each orbiter subsystem using checklists similar to those used on an actual mission.

Following that part of the training, astronauts begin working in the complex shuttle mission simulators (SMSs). This is where they are trained in all areas of shuttle vehicle operations and systems tasks associated with major space flights: from prelaunch and ascent to orbit operations, entry, and landing. The orbit training includes payload operation, payload deployment and retrieval, maneuvers, and rendezvous. In the simulators, a digital image-generation system depicts the visual images the astronauts will see throughout the mission—the Earth, stars, payloads, and the landing runway. In other words, a space shuttle mission is simulated from launch to landing.

Once astronauts are assigned to a particular mission—usually about ten months before the flight—they begin training on computer software similar to that to be used on the flight. They get the actual flight software for training about eleven weeks before the mission.

During those last eleven weeks, the astronauts also train with the flight controllers at the Mission Control Center. The training facility is linked to the center the same way the spacecraft and center are linked during an actual mission. This way the astronauts and controllers learn to work as a team, solving problems and working out procedures and timelines for particular activities of that mission.

Another weightless environment astronauts train in is a huge water tank that contains a mockup of the shuttle orbiter payload bay and various payloads. *Payload* is the term used for items carried by the spacecraft that are directly related to the flight mission (passengers, instruments, spare parts) as opposed to things needed just for operation of the space shuttle (such as fuel). Underwater, the astronauts wear space suits (extravehicular mobility units) that are made neutrally buoyant. This reduces the sensation of gravity and provides a very close simulation of the actual working environment in space.

The astronauts also practice space mission tasks, ranging from meal preparation and trash management to the use of cameras and equipment stowage, in several full-scale mock-ups and trainers. They also participate in test and checkout activities at the NASA Kennedy Space Center in Florida, from where space shuttles are launched.

Astronauts have commented that only the noise and vibration of the liftoff and launch of the shuttle and the actual prolonged experience of weightlessness are missing from the practice sessions; everything else in training accurately duplicates the real space experience.

Opportunities in NASA

There are basically three astronaut specialties you can apply for: commander/pilot, mission specialist, or payload specialist.

Commander/pilot astronauts serve as both space shuttle commanders and pilots. During flight, the commander has full responsibility for the spacecraft, crew, mission success, and safety of the flight.

The pilot assists the commander in controlling and operating the vehicle and may assist in deploying and retrieving satellites using the remote manipulator system—the robot arm that operates out of the payload bay of the shuttle orbiter.

Mission specialist astronauts have overall responsibility for coordinating shuttle operations in the following areas: crew activity planning, consumables usage, and experiment/payload operations. They are trained in the details of the orbiter onboard systems and in the operational characteristics, requirements and objectives, and supporting equipment and systems for each of the space experiments to be conducted on the mission. Mission specialists also perform EVAs—extra-vehicular activities, or space walks. Now that's a trip!

Payload specialists are persons other than NASA astronauts who have specialized onboard duties. They may be foreign nationals. They may be added to shuttle crews if activities with unique requirements are involved in the mission and more than the minimum crew of five persons is needed.

Qualified NASA mission specialists are given first consideration for these additional crew member positions. And when payload specialists are required, they are nominated by NASA, the foreign sponsor, or the designated payload sponsor. Although the payload specialists are not necessarily part of the astronaut program, they must have had the appropriate education and training required for the payload experiment, and they must pass NASA space physical exams.

Your Future as an Astronaut

Today aspiring astronauts compete with an average of thirty-five hundred candidates for about twenty jobs as mission specialists or pilot astronauts that open every two years. The primary requirements are a bachelor of science degree in engineering, science, or math (advanced degrees are desirable) and experience related to the field. For additional requirements, contact the Johnson Space Center in Houston.

The space shuttle continues to be NASA's workhorse vehicle for hauling people and cargo to the space station and into Earth's orbit. Astronauts aboard the space station perform space activities and experiments plus construction and maintenance work. The station is an orbiting laboratory for microgravity experiments in fluid dynamics, production of new and improved metals and alloys, and biotechnology research. Crews also investigate the medical effects of long-duration stays in zero gravity and test new robotic technology.

With the great leaps in technology at the start of this century, there is talk of developing pilotless space vehicles to take astronauts to the space station and beyond. For now, if you join the astronaut corps, your annual salary will be based on the federal government's General Schedule pay scales. For astronauts, these pay scales range from grades GS-11 to GS-14, or about $43,000 to $93,000 a year, depending on your education and experience. Military astronauts are paid by the service branch according to the rank and time in service. Civilian applicants apply to:

NASA, Johnson Space Center
Astronaut Selection Office
Mail Code AHX
2101 NASA Road 1
Houston, TX 77058
www.jsc.nasa.gov

Active-duty military candidates must submit applications to their service branches.

For More Information

National Aeronautic and Space Administration
www.nasajobs.nasa.gov/jobs/astronauts/aso_sp2.htm

American Institute of Aeronautics and Astronautics
1801 Alexander Bell Drive, Suite 500
Reston, VA 20191
www.aiaa.org

Adventurers and Hangers-On

Throughout history, a small number of people we call adventurers seek extreme challenges in their travels. They climb forbidding mountains, attempt to break flight records in hot air balloons and solo airplane trips, take on daring ocean sailing challenges, and seek space travel as tourists. In April 2001, California businessman Dennis Tito became the first American to travel in space as a tourist. He paid $20 million for his ticket aboard a Russian Soyuz spacecraft to the International Space Station, where he spent six days. "I love space," he said when he arrived at the space station. And in May 2002, South African Internet millionaire Mark Shuttleworth paid more than $1 million to travel by Russian spacecraft to the International Space Station for a ten-day space voyage before returning to earth in the Soyuz capsule.

Slightly less daring people have made packaged adventure treks among the most popular items on the menus of tour companies.

Lastly, there are persons who, by dint of blind luck, creative savvy, or ingenious scheming, work their way into positions that allow them to fulfill the quest for endless world travel on the coattails of others. For example, the guy who drives the bus for road tours of the hottest rock band; the bodyguard who goes wherever the famous screen star travels; the agent/manager for the famous entertainer or business mogul who must always have a servant just a few steps away.

Who can tell how far the quest for travel excitement and fulfillment in a career will take you? Maybe you will create an entirely new job that will be your magic carpet!

CHAPTER NINE

How to Find *Your* Traveling Job

A s a practical matter, finding a job that involves travel calls for the same techniques and strategies you would use to search for any kind of job. But being a travel buff may give you an edge in some cases because, for many people, business travel is not attractive. Indeed, they may avoid jobs that require traveling.

Conducting a job search is a difficult task that requires a lot of skill, enterprise, and energy. Most of us go through the process of looking for a job only sporadically in our working lifetimes. A reasonably successful person might change jobs only six or seven times in thirty-five years of work.

So, since this task is probably somewhat foreign to you, take the time to study it before you dive in. There are dozens of books on how to conduct a successful job search; get one and read through it. Following are some of the tips you're likely to find in most job-hunting books:

• **Lay the groundwork for your search.** Compose a resume that presents a comprehensive but quick survey of your experience and accomplishments. Try to keep it to a page, two at most. Your resume doesn't have to detail your life history; its purpose is to get you in the door at a company —to get you invited to an interview. You don't get jobs from resumes. You can only get a job from an interview.

In order to get those interviews, you'll have to do some research on the employment scene in your community and others where the kind of job you want exists. Consult job banks offered by associations you may belong to, check out major online job websites such as monster.com and hotjobs.com, and comb business directories and other resources at your local library for names of companies and other organizations that have the kinds of jobs you seek. Get names of appropriate managers at companies with jobs you want, then write or E-mail them about a job. Also check the help-wanted ads in your local newspaper and in journals and publications in your target career field.

- **Practice for your interviews.** Get a friend to act as an employer and interview you, so you can figure out how to react to different questions and situations. Common sense will tell you a lot about how to handle an interview—be on time, dressed for business, and well groomed. Bone up on the company before you go for the interview, so you'll be able to ask some intelligent questions and respond knowledgeably to the interviewer's inquiries. Don't argue with the interviewer. Don't badmouth other employers or jobs. Take with you samples of your work and other materials an employer might want to see.

  The real key is to be relaxed and comfortable with the situation. If you are, the back-and-forth exchange between you and the interviewer will probably be quite conversational—normal—and that will demonstrate that you interact well with other people. And communicating well is a major criterion for any job.

- **Network.** Tell everyone you know that you are looking for a job. You never can tell when one of them may hear of something and let you know. Many people find their jobs through word of mouth and networking among friends and business colleagues. Follow up every lead you get about a job, even if it doesn't sound all that promising at first. At the very least, it may give you a chance to practice your interview technique. And, if you're lucky, it could turn out to be the job of your dreams.

- **Persevere.** Finding a job can take time. The higher the level of the job and the pay, the longer it can take. It's easy to get discouraged when you don't get calls you hoped for or replies to your inquiries. But keep your spirits up. In my book, *30 Days to a Good Job* (Simon & Schuster), my coauthor and I suggest plotting out a detailed thirty-day schedule for your job hunt—even to allowing time for exercise each day and goals for getting target numbers of resumes mailed.

Eventually everybody who wants a job finds one. Landing the particular job you want, one that lets you travel, may take longer than you thought. And you may have to take a circuitous course—for instance, by accepting a different but related job in order to be in a position to move into the job you really want at a later time. As a travel buff, when you find that perfect job, the wait will have been worth it.

About the Author

··

Paul Plawin has been a journalist and writer for forty years. He began his career as a newspaper reporter, then he moved to magazines and spent more than twenty-four years as an editor with *Southern Living, New Orleans, Better Homes & Gardens,* and *Kiplinger's Personal Finance* magazines. He covered court trials, police raids, and the military in his newspaper days. As a magazine editor, he wrote about subjects ranging from small business and career strategies to travel and leisure lifestyles. He is a past president of the Society of American Travel Writers. He is married, has two children and five grandchildren, and now writes books, columns, and content for websites as a freelancer. He lives on the outskirts of Washington, D.C., in Gainesville, Virginia. He also is the author of *30 Days to a Good Job* (Simon & Schuster).